The Voice of an Angel is a warm, compassionate guide for any parent that has experienced the unspeakable grief of losing a child. Marcy is a remarkable example of courage and grace in the face of intense pain, as she takes the reader by the hand and leads them on a path toward hope and healing. May God bless Marcy for sharing her wisdom for how to cope with life's most difficult tragedy. The journey never ends, but having someone with whom to share it makes it more bearable than it otherwise would be.

David Fox, M.D.,
Author of Comfort, Healing, and Joy: Secrets to Living
a Magnificent Life

The Voice of an Angel provides a road map for any mother who has experienced a sudden and tragic loss of her child. The coping mechanisms Marcy uses to deal with her unbelievable loss can also be applied to everyday life and the message here is simple; LOVE. Marcy reminds us to live by simple and easy to understand principles and have faith, as hard as it may be sometimes, and life will be much more beautiful.

Sgt. Daniel Mulligan, Head of the Crash,
Analysis and Reconstruction Unit

With the energetic whispers of the spirit of Sydney from the other side, this mother daughter partnership reveals an easier way to travel through and experience that, which is in all respects far from easy. "The Voice of an

Angel" is a beautiful testament to a brave, courageous and determined mother who refused to allow her biggest tragedy to break her and instead rebirthed her in a stronger wiser and more present version of herself.

Jo Jayson Intuitive Artist, Teacher and Author of the award winning book Self-Love through the Sacred Feminine - A guide to self-love through the paintings and channeling of Jo Jayson

This is a "must read" for anyone who has lost a loved one. Marcy provides concrete guidance and support for all of our feelings, emotions and thoughts. She shows us how to navigate our lives, allowing the love of our "lost one" to flow through us, thus never really being lost or forgotten. This book is a powerful tool for navigating loss and grief and reclaiming a joyous life.

Karolee Schloth, M. Ed. Spiritual Teacher and Guide

"The Voice of an Angel" is a very warm and touching book with so much empowering content. Understanding and learning that grief is different for everyone and embracing the tools that Marcy brings to the table, helps to navigate and feel valid in how we see ourselves through this journey. Her total honesty and vulnerability allowed me to process through the emptiness that has been left behind in losing my son. As I am four years into my process, this books techniques' to navigating this journey has helped me feel like maybe I haven't totally lost my mind.

Susan Childers

ISBN: 9781718165199

Cover & Interior Design by: Walter Stanley of Stanley Graphic Arts

Author's photo courtesy of: Aubrey Nicole Riegel

The Voice of an Angel

DEDICATION

To all that walk by my side on this journey

The Voice of an Angel

A Mother's guide to
grief and loss and
how to thrive
after the loss of a child

Marcy Stone

Table of Contents

The Voice of an Angel

Introduction

Why I wrote this

When my daughter was still alive, she would make crazy concoctions in the kitchen and she would tease and say, *"just you watch momma, some day you're going to see my name in lights"*. Soon after she was killed, she would visit me in my dreams and share things with me: some to help me understand, some to show me she was doing well and others were messages to help me through the long process ahead of me. She showed me all the ways she was going to stay in contact with me going forward and told me I would never be alone. As I write this, her messages guide me through how to offer you comfort, direction and the same thing she did for me, letting you know you are not alone. To name this book *"The Voice of an Angel"* seemed only too appropriate and my way of giving her the wish of seeing her name in lights, so to speak.

I believe mothers are made extra resilient. We are physically designed to carry a child and give birth. We spend the first 18+ years of our sweet baby's life raising them and molding them into the magical being they become. Then we are asked to let them go into the world and separate that second umbilical cord we energetically have attached to them. Yet gratefully, they willingly allow us to continue to mentor and love from whatever distance they choose. We catch them if they fall and always have outstretched arms lovingly awaiting the next hug and kiss on the cheek. We never judge them and know they take every word we say as gospel. So we choose our words wisely and continue to live as an example.

We are then sometimes asked to call upon that momma bear resiliency to face our worst nightmare...

You are not alone. Through this book you can find your way through the despair and emptiness that consumes you. I have walked a similar path and experienced that same deafening silence in my soul. With my Angel's help I was able to create these guidelines. They will hopefully provide you the ability to take a few good deep breaths and feel okay not being okay in the initial part of this journey.

Some guidelines to follow

As I was writing this, I was provided the unfortunate opportunity to re-test, yet again, this process. It came about as a direct result of the criminal trail related to the death of my daughter. Needless to say, the grief wheel you will see depicted in later chapters was challenged and proven accurate. As I was organizing my thoughts to share with you as clearly as I could, I came to understand a few things differently. Each of the steps in the wheel will always be within us going forward. How we manage to harness the love we hold for both ourselves and our lost love will help determine just how muted each of them feels or manifests as situations in life arise.

Another potentially unfortunate reality is that if we are not extremely mindful, we have the propensity to fall into one reactionary emotion. This means it becomes our "go to" reaction before we rationally assess and then behave accordingly. For a period of time, and especially at the one-year milestone, anger was becoming my go to emotion. I would feel myself bubbling over like a teapot and explode, even over things that would not normally warrant a reaction. Even with the guidance of my Angel, it took me time to get a handle on allowing myself to feel the actual emotion the anger was protecting me from. It was usually the deep feeling I was dodging. The voice of my Angel says to me, *"Momma, feel the pain, lean into it. Find the love, that is what will get you through"*...this was a mantra for quite a long time and I find it visits me often, still. So, staying present in the pain and allowing yourself to feel all that flows

4

through you, honoring it and what it represents within you will be a very large piece of this healing process. Paying attention to what your "go to" emotion is will help you stay present and find balance. This will allow you to feel the correct emotion vs. your go to emotion.

Now is not a time to become indecisive, with the exception of the first week or so. After that I urge you to stay in the game and continue to make decisions based on what you are feeling at the time. The people around you will counsel you on what they feel is best both for you and for the time at hand. Ultimately you still know what is best for you. Please remain present for you, for your loved ones still walking this plane with you and also for your beautiful baby that is now an Angel watching over you. Make them all proud and show them that you will make as much goodness happen to honor them, to honor what they mean to you. This will also show yourself that in time you can still live and feel good again.

As time ticks by you will see a new reality unfold. You will have a better understanding as to why I ask you to please remain attentive and present throughout all of the pain and to harness the love. This new reality that unfolds is yours to shape and design. How you decide to move forward will be instrumental in your ability to find happiness again and yes, it really is possible.

The flow of this book

Logic would say that in the beginning of a process you would choose your intention (what you aspire to do or be), your goal (what your outcome will look like) and in this situation, (how you want to get there), meaning what kind of "warrior" do you want to be through this process.

However, there is absolutely nothing logical about grief or how you may navigate it. Simply by choosing to read this book you have already made a step towards these very thoughts, probably not intentionally. You just want to stop suffering and for the pain to stop. What you will find as you read is the process I uncovered directly following my daughters funeral. So, the order is intrinsic.

I share this with you because if you are reading this and you are further along in your grief process, you might be wondering about the flow of the chapters. That is totally understandable. As I look back on the flow, I was tempted to move the information regarding the 3 Warriors to the beginning of the book BUT, that felt wrong to me. Wrong to my journey, wrong to those that are also finding this in the early stages of their grief and I need to honor that feeling. If you are in the first months of losing your sweet baby and I start telling you to choose what kind of warrior you want to be, your first response (before throwing the book out!) will be, "YOU'VE GOT TO BE JOKING! I DON'T WANT TO BE HERE AT ALL, LET ALONE CHOOSE HOW I AM GOING TO DO IT!" Well, that's what I would

The Voice of an Angel

have said to you if you wrote it. So I am honoring how I went through the process.

For those of you that are further in your grief and are starting to feel and see some things logically again, **congratulations**. That is beautiful and I am proud of you for allowing yourself to be there. For you, I will briefly share the warriors here so you can take this journey in a more logical fashion.

The 3 Warriors are the Crusader Warrior, Surviving Warrior and the Thriving Warrior they are defined in greater detail in Chapter 7.

Please, keep in mind; no matter where you are in your grief, you have the opportunity to revisit these 3 warriors along with everything else I lay out for you. Change it, as it feels right to you. There is no right or wrong answer, only what serves you best at that moment.

Through this process, may you find yourself thriving through all of your grief and loss. Learn to utilize the love within you to design a beautiful new reality. Find peace within, knowing your sweet child is with you but in new ways and making life not just good but extraordinary. Just lean into the love.

One – If you're reading this, your worst nightmare has come true

There is no greater bond then a momma bear's love for her children. For nine months we are one, breathing the same air, eating the same food, feeling the same feelings and even experiencing the same emotions. This unique and beautiful connection is then compounded when we, as momma bears, are blessed with the day they take their first breath. Their warm, perfect little bodies now for us to explore and ensure that everything is as it should be and that they are healthy. An example being their first breath and disconcerted cry, using those precious lungs and vocal cords of theirs as they express their very first solo functions and emotions. And so it continues, the incredible bond of momma bear and child. It is at that moment, when you look into your sweet baby's eyes and you make that silent solemn vow that you will do everything you can to protect them and to give them all they need in this world. You realize that there is no other reason to be alive and you ask yourself, *"What took me so long to decide to become a momma bear?"*

Every "first" in your baby's life, for you, is exhilarating with moments of terrifying, sometimes mixed in, but again, you wouldn't trade it for anything. As they grow, they demonstrate their little personalities and their interests and you slowly realize not only are you their teacher but you are their student. Through watching them and seeing what they need, you realize and learn how to help them understand the balance of things: letting them fall vs. coddling them, choice and consequence, truth vs. rationalize, lead vs. follow, listen vs. watch, right vs. wrong, love vs. hate, etc. Every moment, every breath they take simply captivates you and it's beautiful at every level for those that cherish the momma bear, child relationship.

As our children grow, we need to give them their space to utilize the wisdom we have instilled over the years. Some through living by example and some by listening to what they need and what is important to them. The time has come to let them spread their wings. They explore and experience the world and to your delight, your sweet child is happy to return to embrace you as if they were seven again, with that sweet innocence that is like a drug to a momma bear. You just can't seem to get enough of their love and the beauty of their presence and they still regard you as the best momma bear ever! That just never gets old and can still bring a tear to your eye. You find yourself occasionally daydreaming, wondering what they will be when they grow into the person they are becoming? Will they get married? Have children? Maybe start their own business? But then you come back to the moment and are happy you don't have those things too close to contend with because each moment of today is really just wonderful and you wouldn't trade a thing. LIFE IS BEAUTIFUL.

The next thing you know, the pit of your stomach, your throat, and your heart...your entire body feels like it is shutting down and you can't breathe. The room around you feels like it is spinning and, in the distance, somewhere you hear voices but can't make out what anyone is saying. You keep telling yourself this all has to be a bad dream or a mistake. There is no way my baby can be gone. As quickly as those thoughts are flashing through your mind you also instantly start with thoughts of how can this be, how will I survive, what do I do...and then go blank, with no thoughts at all. Just a numb blurry silence and there you want to stay. Its safe here and there is no pain and then someone startles you by putting their hand on your shoulder and says, *"is there someone I can call for you?"* That single statement brings you back to reality and in that next second you remember the rest of your family. More than ever, they will need to know and they will look to you for how to get through this unspeakable tragedy.

You flash back to all of your sweet baby's "firsts" throughout their precious life and now, there will be no more firsts for them. All of a sudden, somehow, somewhere in the next however many minutes that pass, you seem to find this strength. Your "momma bear gene" kicks into autopilot and you muster the ability to stand and speak again and just in time! In through the door comes the other people in the world that look to you for advice or for courage or for guidance and this is absolutely going to be one of those moments. They are going to count on what you can bring to the situation to help make some sense of all of this and even at times help them understand how to feel and how to process what is transpiring second by second. This is an incredible power bestowed upon momma bears and one not to be taken lightly. How you react, speak and move will be how the other people you love will also behave. They emulate you and know you will know what to do. **They count on you knowing what to do.** If only they knew that you felt like you were dying inside and couldn't breathe!   Then you think to yourself, I can grieve and be strong so that the rest of my family will see the balance between the two and find a healthy way to move through this. For a split second you wonder how you can be having such sane, organized and rational thoughts at a time like this. This is the first of many moments in the pinball process of grief.

Perhaps this is how it felt for you and maybe it was harder, uglier, more devastating and you have every right to feel exactly like you do and for as long as you need. Not everyone has had the misfortune of losing a child and there is no one that can compare his or her pain, experience or situation. What someone else thinks or feels is irrelevant to you and please don't allow someone to try to compare the loss of their uncle or cousin to what it is that you are experiencing. There is no comparison. Period, end of story. **How you are feeling is exactly how you need to feel so feel no shame, but PLEASE be sure to feel.**

Grieve your way

Unfortunately, most people don't know what to say when someone dies or is killed. They freeze up and often times either say something and they seem to feel ridiculous or are filled with anger or they try to say something positive and uplifting. And all you are probably trying to do is stop yourself from telling them to go keep their opinions to themselves!

While I had all of what I listed above, I am of a little different mold than most people so something I did and found to be very therapeutic was at my daughter's funeral. I invited people to do those very things I listed above. I explained to everyone that I understood that people were not going to know how to react around me and would struggle with what to say so they might be inclined to avoid me.

In allowing this for them, it made the occasional awkward moments or comments not as painful or difficult because I invited it and was open to how they needed to express themselves. Death is not an easy subject for anyone but especially when the death is of such a young, vibrant and beautiful child. I would rather someone stumble through saying something, then avoid me. I would also expect them to be uncomfortable and be grateful that it was not them that was in my place. I asked them to be okay with that feeling because it is perfectly normal and understandable.

I invited them to do what they could and to be okay with that. I also requested that no one send negative or evil thoughts towards the man that is responsible for taking Sydney's life. He has a long hard road ahead of him and then he has his karma. To send him ugliness only hurts the individual sending the energy.

I share this so you can see what listening to your gut seems like at even one of the most tragic events in a momma bear's life. I share it so you understand you can give yourself the permission to do what you need during this journey, starting with the message you send out to the world. This is your life and this is your baby we are all mourning and you have a say in how it is going to be handled from this moment on.

Things I would have liked someone to prepare me for

Now you are past the funeral and trying to figure out what to do day by day and it may be starting to get quiet again. There seems to be a societal time limit on grieving, sad but true. The first 10 days or so people call, stop by, send cards and check on you, offering support and then they slowly drift back into their own lives. They love us and they love our baby but they are not connected like we are, so life starts happening again for them. They then tend to text or call every couple of weeks to see how you're doing and when they hear you are still so incredibly grief stricken some of them will appear puzzled or even put off. They can't seem to understand why you aren't doing any better by now. Because they don't understand and maybe even consider you weak or lingering in your grief, they distance themselves.

Then you have the angry grievers, (not saying you are not angry), and their form of consoling you is by venting their anger about their loss of your child and how it devastates them. You are then left to console them! While they really mean well and are reaching out because they genuinely care about you, they have so much of their own anger to contend with that when they speak with you it comes out full force. You may just be the one that does the distancing in this particular case.

Then you have the people that when they see you at the store and you look seemingly put together, and its only been 3 months since the funeral, they shockingly wave and say hi and something like, "I'm surprised to see you out and about". This is again where I say to you, please do what you need and move about the country, so to speak, how you need to for you. Don't let these people shame you for how you need to move forward and the timing in which you need to do so. This is your journey. You will recalibrate and identify with who you are becoming and what your new reality is going to entail.

Healing grief

Before I knew what I was talking about, I always thought you could heal grief. Everything has a shelf life, right? Maybe you would cry some, feel bad for a while and then a time would come when you would be better and get back on with your life, as you knew it, like you had recovered from the flu. Then a few years ago, I consoled a friend that lost their spouse and seeing their pain, I realized that is absolutely unequivocally not the case. Now, having experienced the worst tragedy I can ever imagine and finding myself in all stages of grief, I have come to better understand there is no real solution or fix, to healing grief. It is something that now becomes a part of who we are and we have the choice of how we allow it to shape or mold us.

Another ah-ha moment for me as I walk this unpaved path, is while grief is a combination of many mixed emotions, as time passes **the remaining emotion that will always be there is love**. You can experience anger, regret, disbelief, deep sorrow and over time each one of these, if navigated in healthy ways, can be resolved, healed, or lessened over time until they fade, but love never disappears. I have come to understand that the love that is felt for the person you are grieving for has no place to go, no individual to share it with on this plane and so you have all of this love in your heart and soul and nowhere to take it. You are overflowing with love and it hurts so very deeply because it's so vast and pure. This, I believe is why my Sydney said *"feel the pain momma"*, its giving the love a place to go initially and then as the other emotions seem to settle, the love is what has been keeping you fueled, so to speak. It has been carrying you through the grief, giving it a new purpose and a place to channel it vs. the physical being you would love to hug and hold right now. It is not a fabulous option. It is the one I would choose over closing my heart to this love I feel for my beautiful sweet child instead of becoming hard and cold and distant to the rest of my loved ones, family and friends. Your sweet baby is saving your life with the love you have for them as it, while painful, carries you through the next months and slowly starts to feel more enduring and pure.

Hanging on

If you are anything like me, you are going to do everything you can think of to make sure your sweet little mini-me is going to be remembered and cherished for the rest of your life! Quite honestly, nothing makes you feel better right now then telling stories about how sweet your baby was, hearing other people's stories about what they remember and finding "keepsake" ways of having them close to you. You might start out by making things like pillows from favorite t-shirts or blankets or maybe a mosaic of their artwork or silly doodles they did over the years. Whatever the project, it doesn't matter, as long as you feel close to them.

Whether you need to paint a mural after 3 months to honor the loss of your beloved child or you need to start a foundation after 6 months or if you even need to wait and have a celebration in honor of your baby on their birthday, it is extremely important that you listen to what you need to do for you. It does not matter what anyone else says, so don't give them an audience to offer their point of view. Most people think that you should pull the blinds, live in darkness, wear black and can't smile or have a happy moment for at least the first year of loss. THAT IS YOUR CHOICE. You have all kinds of choices now and moving forward. Choose what you want, not what others are prescribing.

Baby steps but still forward

I am so very sorry for the loss you are experiencing and the pain that feels embedded throughout your entire being. I truly believe that there is no pain greater. Please know that is why I created this for you. I am extremely compassionate and sympathetic of how delicate you are currently, but I also know that you have a warrior within you. That very warrior is going to enable you to survive at first and then in time, thrive.

Throughout this book you will be asked to call upon that warrior to be strong, while still honoring where you are in your journey. There will be challenges asked of you, taking you out of your comfort zone, if even for a second, to experience and create your own way through this devastating loss. What worked for me may not be what moves you, but through this process, you will identify what resonates with you and forge your path so in time you will feel like life is worth living again. Once you make the choice of life vs. lifelessness, perhaps your "muchness" ("more than life", unique, quirky and extraordinary personality) will return and that warrior will lead you to what awaits you in the next chapter of your life.

A thread of hope

I would like to share a poem that a friend of mine wrote for me within the first days of losing my daughter. It was amazing to me how he was able to capture some of what I was feeling and how his words seemed to give me the permission to grieve the way I needed to. It also gave me confirmation in a sense that she was, in fact, happy and smiling down upon me. Now, with his permission, I share his words with you in hopes to provide you with similar comfort and a thread of hope.

Your twin star, your happy sidekick
Sadly taken away too soon
Grieve as you must
Then allow the healing to begin
She is dancing in the music between the spheres
Awaiting assignment to her next adventure

Now what?

I am going to introduce some concepts throughout the following chapters, things that truly helped me find my way. I will ask you to take a leap of faith and choose now, in the beginning of this unchartered path you begrudgingly find yourself in, WHO you want to be, HOW can you dream or imagine yourself getting there and WHAT could this new you look like at the end of this tunnel of painstaking grief. Every chapter will build on how to help you find your way and bring this potential vision of you to life, and YES...it really is possible. It will take time and like me, you will stumble...often, but it is absolutely 100% better than the alternative. I cannot imagine sitting in my sorrow, feeling sorry for myself, letting down those that love me and look to me for support. There is zero chance of me wanting to look up to the heavens and saying out loud, "I can't do this". **I will not live in darkness.** Sydney knows that I can do this. I know I can do this. I know you can do this.

My hope for you is that you first, find some peace and to not feel so alone and lost. Secondly, as time passes, I hope you will find the motivation and inspiration to figure out how to thrive through this grief and feel good again knowing your sweet child wants you to sparkle. They also want you to be all that you can be and to live an extraordinary life, so let's get started!

Two – My journey in becoming a Thriving Warrior

Attempting to comprehend the surreal... the knock on the door

There are no words for the feeling that surface when there is a knock on the door and when you open it, there are two police officers on the other side. Your mind immediately starts to race along with the beat of your heart. Thoughts like they have to have the wrong house and why me, all come at once, come fast and furious, still not even sure why they are there. Then when you finally hear their words, feelings of despair, disbelief and feeling sick to your stomach, are your immediate reactions, as you fight it and try to let it sink in all at the same time. The officer explains things like "no identification" and "identify her by her tattoo"... the room is spinning and the chair you are on seems to be rocking as you are doubled over in indescribable pain.

It's all so surreal, yet the officer continues to offer his condolences while asking if there is anyone he can call to come be with me. I see his lips moving and hear words but they still are not forming a sentence I am able to comprehend. I hand him my phone and he is now speaking to someone on my phone yet I don't recall bringing up a number for him. He is reiterating a version of the horror I am still trying to swallow. I can't catch my breath and as I apologize for crying and try to remember my manners (seriously?) offering them a glass of water, he says something else. I think it was an effort to calm me, and now I can no longer keep it down and I excuse myself because I am going to be sick.

This cannot be happening to me, to my precious beloved baby, sidekick, partner in crime, love of my life... and as if that isn't bad enough...its Christmas Eve day. I don't know how long I am upstairs but as my fiancé arrives and he is reaching for me, grabbing me tight, his face is that of such grief and disbelief, knowing and feeling every ounce of my pain. All he wants to do is take my pain away, make this all go away for all of us but mostly for my Syd'y. We wanted her back so desperately, yet not really even completely digesting that we will never see her, feel her, hear her ever again.

As I gather myself the best I can, we proceed back down to the reality I was running from and my older daughter and her husband arrive. I am not sure who called them but they arrived in shock and tearful. She runs to me and hugs me fiercely with hopes that I will tell her not to worry, and it was all a mistake and our Sydney is perfectly okay. This is sorrowfully something I am unable to give her.

We are asked to go to the hospital to identify my daughter's body. Again, another slam to the solar plexus...the permanent reality of that terrible statement..."identify my daughter's body". Once again, I broke down but still thinking, please let this all be a terrible mistake, all the while knowing deep within my core that my Sydney was gone from this earth. At that instant, and many others since then, I have floods of flashbacks of incredible memories. Memories that are all joy filled, full of love and life and laughter. All my memories of my two daughters and I, of being inseparable and enjoying relationships that most momma bears and daughters do not have the privilege to experience, we were (and are) truly blessed. So much love, honor and respect for each other.

The four of us, quietly drove to the hospital, still with the slightest ray of hope that it might not be her. That final moment of denial we all knew to be fruitless, yet realized it was allowing us to continue to breath. The hospital was very kind and tried to prepare us for what we were about to witness. At that moment I was provided an out. I was told, "*you don't need to do this*" but every ounce of my being as a mother...no a momma bear, friend, confidant and human being knew I would forever regret it if I did not experience that visual closure. Seeing my baby one last time and feeling the pain she felt in her last moment. As they guided us into the room where she lay peacefully, all I could do was cry. I hugged her cold lifeless body and kissed her cheek one last time, as the truth of her being was gone, no longer able to incubate. IT WAS NOW FACT.

The next few hours are a complete blur. I remember the boys going to get her car. I remember making calls to family members to inform them and going to the funeral home (it was Christmas eve day, my family was to celebrate together that afternoon). I don't know what happened after that or the following day. I recall people stopping over to pay their respects and share stories of how Sydney touched their lives and how they will forever be changed. I remember going through pictures and crying at every devilish smile and her glittering, teasing eyes. She was so beautiful inside and outside.

The reality of the moment seemed like it was sinking in and then in the next I was suffocating. I didn't know if I was going to make it to the next minute, let alone the next hour. As the funeral is planned, friends jumped in to help arrange pictures, slides, etc...it really is all so surreal and a blur. People asked about songs and did we want to have a reception following the funeral. No! I want my daughter back and all of this to just evaporate into a horrific dream. Because of the holiday, a few days had to pass before we were able to have the funeral. I remember wondering if Sydney would approve of what I chose to wear and I cried. I cried at every thought, every comment and every hug. I, too, wanted to die that day and many days following.

What makes me tick

The funeral lasted for what felt like forever but what got me through that day and every day after, are these two things; I decided that morning that I had two reasons to live. Just two.

My oldest daughter, who needs me now more than ever and needs to see how to survive this tragedy and keep living and the other was Sydney's voice in my head saying, *"I'm safe, I'm sorry, I love you. Please live a beautiful life and I will be with you every step of the way"*. These are my raisons d'etre, my reasons for living.

I always said that having my girls saved my life, saved me from myself. I wasn't on any particularly healthy paths at that time in my life and my girls, over the years, made me realize just how precious life really was. They taught me how to love and how to forgive and how to be my best self. Over time I realized that through wanting to be the best person, momma, role model and mentor I could be for my girls, I allowed them to show me the way. They have always been and always will be my raison d'etre. Now I have one watching over me in heaven and one walking by my side.

My relationship with my daughter, then and now

As the hours passed and everyone came to say hello and offer a story or a tearful hug, I realized that I knew every single person that came through that line, and as we spoke, I was reminded of just how close Sydney and I were. Some of the things people were saying to me were stories that I was now hearing their version of, because I already knew Sydney's version. Sydney and I were so incredibly close that her friends knew me as, *"my momma, my best friend"*. I took great pride in that. The girls and I really were a fabulous trio. Aubrey was a little more like a beautiful, independent cat in that she would come around when she wanted love and attention and then was happy to go off and explore the world as she needed and saw fit. I was like that when I was young so I totally understood, respected it and honored her ways. But make no mistake, she was and is very attentive and knows when I need(ed) her too.

Sydney, however, was a lap dog. She and I were always together and she would tease and say she was going to be with me until I was 95 and that made me perfectly happy. My girls are my world and that was always very clear to them.

When they were both young, I was given a message that Sydney would not be with us forever. It was a jolt to say the least but I am a woman of faith, in that I listen to the guidance I am provided. So, having received that incredibly scary yet profound information, I did some soul digging. It was at that moment I made the girls and myself a promise, that we would make every moment count. We would live a life with no regrets, and that's what we did. So, on that fateful day when Sydney was tragically taken from me, from us, little did we know that we did all that we could together and in doing so, it saved our lives, our hearts and our souls.

What I mean by this is that we lived a life together with no regrets. We said what we needed, spent quality time together, didn't let things get in our way of being our true selves, we were honest with each other, let go of what didn't really matter and had no secrets. Now that's not to say that with three women in the house that tempers didn't flare. When that did happen, it was usually Aubrey and I and it was always Sydney the peacemaker, that would come to our rescue singing, *"why can't we be friends"*. She never got past the first verse and Aubrey and I would crack up laughing and all was well with the world again. We lived a truly remarkable life together.

Over the first six months or so following the funeral, I would have the most vivid dreams. Dreams of Sydney coming to visit me and she would share messages with me and she would show me some of the most beautiful places (she loved to travel). She told me that I would be writing this and said that the world needed a new way to approach loss. I would wake and take notes of each one of these dreams because I never wanted to forget them or how she looked or what she was wearing. I held onto each one of them and knew what she was doing. She was preparing me for the next leg of my journey. The one where I was here and she was there and showing me ways we would "stay in touch". While they still occur, the dreams started to have more distance between them and her "visits" became things like songs at just the right time or a feather or a billboard with a message with just what I was thinking about or wondering. Sometimes I can even find myself in a daydream and receive some amazing message and it always ends with, *"momma, stay present"*, with that giggle I remember soooo well. Sydney sometimes visits friends of mine to check in and let them know she is okay and to give me a message. She liked my friends and thought of them as her own. All of this "contact" helped keep me in check and stay moving forward and able to feel the love in my heart, which was so very broken and raw. Every time I had a moment where I didn't think I could go on, I very deliberately took myself back to my raison d'etre. There were days that I took myself back to that thought so many times that I didn't think about anything else! However over time, the hours became minutes. Now I have sad or bad moments in good days vs. bad days consumed with sad moments. All because of my raison d'etre.

I'd like take a moment to share a little of my Sydney with you so you can get a sense of her from a partial journal entry I wrote on her first birthday I had without her, September 7, 2017. I am absolutely positive you have incredible stories and memories of your sweet love too. Please share them.

Sydney had a zest for life, she loved to laugh and always new just what to say, no matter what the situation. She had the tendency to undersell herself and the value she added to others, which I believe is how she was able to be as humble as she was.

39
The Voice of an Angel

She LOVED her big sister and hanging out with her, even as they both got older and acted like they bugged each other! They always looked out for each other and every picture I have of the two of them they are arm in arm or just so obviously happy to be together. As they got older, they involved each other in their plans of growth and new chapters (Syd has/had her very own bedroom, you guessed it, aqua blue walls, at her sisters new house)...it was a joy as a momma bear to witness.

She was proud of me and of our relationship and shared our closeness with her friends. As she got older and was interested in stretching her wings, whenever she would get home, she had this amazing way of always making me a part of her adventures and was excited to share with me, ensuring our closeness would always remain.

While she appeared to sometimes have a tough exterior, that was her protection from having been walked out on or let down in the past. It didn't take but a smile and an honest, heartfelt statement from you for her to let you in completely, hook, line and sinker. She loved you vulnerably from this moment on. She would go the distance for anyone she called friend or family and I have heard many stories that consistently prove this statement true, again and again.

Syd had this funny way about her. She was incredibly witty and had the one liners ready like she was reading your mind! She was an antagonist simply because it was fun and I was probably her favorite target! She loved playing to my weaknesses and I loved falling for her ways. She was able to use her wit, with a, sometimes necessary dose of tough love, to tell you what you needed to hear and you always hugged her and thanked her! Never did someone walk away upset or angry. They were grateful that she cared and had a cool way of delivering the, (sometimes painful), message.

The Voice of an Angel

She would always follow up with you later too, to ensure you were good and finding what you needed to keep shining bright! Whether she would have used these words to describe it or not, she loved getting to people's inner light and was a natural at it!

Music was many things for Sydney; healing (not that she would have used that word) and freeing. Her reach of genres was impressive for her age and even at 9 and 10 she was surprising me with her "latest fav". And as I am sure Aubrey would attest to, Sydney would have the lyrics memorized in no time and sing over and over and over and over again, sometimes out of sheer joy and sometimes to get us going! She was an imp to be sure.

Many names did she answer to but one she was proudest of was "the peacemaker". Confrontation, angry words and harsh outcomes were not in her making. She had a way of keeping Aubrey and I "at bay" more than

The Voice of an Angel

once during those famed teenage years and if it was getting loud in the kitchen, Sydney would break into song, "Why can't we be friends, why can't we be friends" and Aubrey and I would just start laughing and just like that the situation was resolved and really didn't seem like that big of a deal any longer. She practiced this uncanny ability with other family and friends too, and I have heard the stories to prove it!

Movies, like music, were something of a passion of Sydney's. She loved learning the soundtracks to movies and often would take the situation or a scene from a movie and relate it to something happening in life. She and her sister share the love of Disney and between them have seen (and maybe even own) the majority of them. They would send each other quotes or pictures of movies just for kicks or so they would know how the other was feeling. They had their own language for sure.

Travel (and the beach!) was something Sydney couldn't get enough of and, because of her grandparents; she had the good fortune of seeing things in the world that most kids her age had not seen. She has been to Russia, Germany, Prague, Bahamas, Mexico, Canada and many US states. She used to tease me to catch up on my traveling! I loved that she and Aubrey were so fortunate and that they were also extremely grateful for having these adventures.

Cousins! ...remembering how important family is and was to Sydney, cousins were also her dear friends and she treasured them so. And cousins of all ages too. She loved the little ones as much as the ones that were her age. She was able to adapt to the younger ones and they loved her so, always feeling that she understood them and she knew exactly what they wanted, needed and how to muster the proper behavior when she would sit for them. I have many pictures of Sydney on the bottom of the pile of

The Voice of an Angel

little kids, everyone having a fabulous time together.

Knowing herself...Sydney was a hard worker but a smart one too. She was fortunate to know at a young age what she was passionate about. The kitchen! Sydney was a foodie to be sure!! She would take crazy things and put them together and it would be strangely tasty. She loved to create in the kitchen and thought that someday she would have her own fusion bar with a wildly creative menu and me tending bar! She figured nothing could go wrong if we did it together!! And I would have been so happy to be a part of her dream. She did try a stent in another field of study, just to see if she was completely sure about the cooking/baking I think, but it was an awesome experience for her and she met some really terrific people during that period of her life. No matter what she was working towards, she worked hard but somehow made it seem effortless.

Her passion – Ultimately, for anyone that knew Sydney, you knew that people were her passion. It brought her great joy to experience people of all ages and stages of life and to get to know them at a depth that most can't do at 50, let alone being in your teens and 20's and doing it so naturally. Her warmth and genuine way of being was something you wanted to be around and somehow absorb and have with you always. She had this uncanny ability to listen, and to hear even what you weren't saying, and then she was able to provide a fun or whimsical way to get you to see things differently that somehow made that obstacle no longer an obstacle. Then you felt able to move through it with a new found confidence. Pretty remarkable. She loved helping people find their happiness and understood it needed to come from within.

There is so so much more to share about Sydney in her 21 years and 3 months of life. But with what I did share, I hope I was able to communicate her winning secret; her heart, her love for all and just the joy she had for being here with us, the people she loved the most. She definitely understood and lived what mattered most to her. She kept life simple, didn't have the need for material stuff, shed what no longer served, called it like she saw it and did what felt right to her soul. She was often my teacher and I will forever be grateful.

Choosing life over lifelessness

There was a time during the first year of losing Sydney that I was trying to identify;

- ♥ Who I was going to be going forward
- ♥ What really mattered to me now
- ♥ And thoughtfully shedding what wasn't working for me anymore

This would help me focus on love and forgiveness for my own long-term sanity and eventual quality of life. It also helped me deal with all of the external changes that were happening to me and around me. It was overwhelming at times and required me to stay present, which wasn't something I always wanted to do because it made me stay in the pain I was feeling. At times it seemed like self-torture, but then I remember hearing Sydney's words, *"stay in the pain momma, as hard as that is to do, so your heart stays open and you can feel love. It's the love you feel that is going to get you through this."* So, I stayed present, did a ton of journaling, reminded myself to breathe, went to an acupuncturist, stayed active in my fitness, listened to what my body needed nutritionally and allowed every emotion to flow without allowing it to consume me. I refused to get caught up in anything that was going to numb my ability to stay present and feel the love. This meant for some long, hard, sad days but from each one of those days I can look back over my journaling and feel the love that comes through in my memories and how those memories started to transform my disposition and mood and the writing would start to turn into a new way to approach life. How blessed we were to have had all that we did and how beautiful life was. Was...

I knew I still hadn't found my "muchness" yet. I tend to be hard on myself, giving myself less time or space than I give everyone else. I got back into my work almost immediately following the funeral. I am a nurturer and a problem solver by nature, so it seemed like the best healing path for me was to help others heal. Heal and be healed was going to be my approach. I created workshops on how to have better relationships with your children. In doing so, the healing was taking place and I felt like I was helping others. Everyone noticed I hadn't gotten my spark or muchness back but most were kind enough not to point it out.

Over time, I found myself able to perform my work in more crystalline ways but my zest for life was still not my usual sparkle. Through the months I did all sorts of healing things that were normal for me; hiking, traveling and helping people, I was finding ways to keep Sydney's memory alive through creating keepsakes, making a Character Album for the District Attorney for the upcoming trial and creating stories or messages on Facebook. However I could share the memory of Sydney, I was going to do so. We then decided to have a "Celebrate her life" gathering for her 22nd birthday in September. We had an aqua blue Adirondack chair made along with a plague to put at the sand pit where she used to work and that's where we had the gathering. I received many mixed reviews on having this event. Some thought it was inappropriate to "celebrate". Others attended and shared their discontent at the event and eventually disappeared from our lives. I knew deep down in my core that I had to have this gathering and on her birthday. It was crucial and I wasn't sure why at the time, but every ounce of my being was saying to do this. So, I listened to my gut and we celebrated Sydney's life. It was beautiful. So many people came from near and far to honor her. They shared stories of things they remembered or things they did together. I was finding strength and a level of resilience that I hadn't had since that fateful morning.

The next morning when I woke up I felt alive and clear, like my muchness was starting to return. I realized at that moment that I had made "the choice". The choice I hadn't realized was waiting for me was, "how was I going to participate in my own life going forward?" That is why one of the reasons my gut was telling me I needed to "celebrate" Sydney's birthday, a milestone. I made the unconscious choice of life over lifelessness. What this means to me is that I chose to get back into my life in every capacity and at my normal level of passion and muchness vs. lack luster and simply surviving. A fun foodie example Syd would have given for that is, *"like rocky road with mint chocolate chip ice cream vs. plain ole' vanilla."*

Why I want to share this and give back

I believe my role on this earth is to give back, serve...through living by example along with the work that I do as a life guide and healer. My passion or purpose in life is to assist people in rediscovering their truest self; changing the energy in their lives by releasing all that hinders them and bring out their inner power for a peace filled life. I also believe that everything good is possible if you have a positive outlook, love in your heart and have good people in your life. I was taught that in order to help people you need to have "walked in their shoes", meaning experience what they are, or have experienced, in order to offer them wisdom. That made perfect sense to me and I have since then joked saying that I have lived the life of a 90 year old. So, the very unfortunate addition of wisdom I am able to add to my toolbox of experience is the tragic and unexpected loss of my daughter. When Sydney came to my dreams, shortly after being taken from me, she told me why she left the way she did. She also provided the other ways she could have left this earth and said that her way was the least painful to me. This didn't mean I wasn't going to grieve, but that I would have closure. She was not going to put me in the situation that I would have to choose life support or free her from her vessel. She also was able to share why she left when she did, at 21 years young and beautiful with so much life to share. She said, *"momma, you did such a good job, I accomplished everything I came into the world to heal and make peace with"*.

Then came her sharing an answer to one of the questions I have been asking myself since that fateful day, *"WHAT DO I DO NOW"*? Sydney proceeded to explain what I was to be doing now with all of this newfound experience and wisdom. *"Momma, help people. It's what you do. There are and will be people, specifically momma bears, that will be grieving the loss of their babies and won't have anywhere "healthy" to turn. The ones that are drawn to what you* write are "difference makers" like you and whether they realize it or not yet, they too, will do things with their lives to be extra-ordinary, in their own way. Be vulnerable and show them what is possible. Show them what it is to love, momma." Well, now how do you say no to a message like that being delivered in a dream by your daughter who is now an Angel watching over you and guiding your every day?

So, by being vulnerable, as my Angel baby has asked, I will share another notation in my journal entries from February 13, 2017.

"Drove by the guys house today. Don't know why or what that would accomplish but I did it anyway. Not at all where I thought it would be because of where the accident was. Leaves me with more questions.

Bagged up Syd'ys clothing that was hanging today. Each piece takes me to a memory, conversation, event, and moment, seeing her *face. Then I just sat on the floor in her room. Don't want to stay but don't want to leave either.*

I can't seem to find that deep, emotional release in order to survive this. I feel like I am moving through but disconnected and numb, if that makes sense. I cry often but there is something deeper that can't seem to find its way out yet. Thinking about this trial and all this guy has taken from me...I can't seem to find an action or emotion that feels...enough."

After creating this journal entry, I lamented for some time feeling all the emotions and stages they say happen when grieving. I realized that now, and probably forever, there will always be unanswered questions and sadness or sorrow in all my days going forward, but I had a choice. I could let this black hole within my heart consume me and go down into a deep, dark place of my days being filled with sadness and sorrow or...I could take this completely awful enormous bag of lemons and make the best damn lemonade I have ever had!! (I use lemons because Sydney used to eat them like they were oranges!) I could choose moments vs. days of sadness and sorrow, finding how to move through this without losing myself. I could instead reinvent myself and start fresh, fueled by our memories and our love.

In looking back over my journal entries and how I felt my way through this I knew, even then, that love was the key. I also knew that forgiveness was another key I was going to need to understand how to maintain my own health and sanity. I mean after all, there is someone standing trial for the death of my daughter. How was I going to move through that process without hating this individual, loathing his entire existence for the remainder of my life?

The following journal entry is from July 23rd...Day 211, our first notification of the criminal trial dates;

My values and beliefs have definitely been questioned through this process, as would any momma bear.

I believe in choice and consequence. Sydney made a choice to trust in the defendant and the consequence was her life. The defendant made a choice to violate her trust, and in so many ways, the angry momma bear within me believes his consequence should be life in prison. That's being completely honest. Is that realistic? I am honestly not sure. Anger is most definitely a huge stage in this process, of both the loss and of the court system, but one that I will not allow myself to become a prisoner to. So as time passes and I flux through all of the stages of emotions that any normal red-blooded human being would experience, I continue reaching within to the depths of my soul, my conscience and my heart. And in between the waves there are moments of silence that are allowing me to realign to my nature self: to what my values and beliefs are and also what I am hearing

Sydney would say to me if she were still here today. She would say something like, "momma, don't let the damage destroy your "rifikiness" (it's a sydney'ism derived from Lion King. It means extraordinariness with a dash of magic & unusual).

So for me, for Sydney and for my oldest daughter, Aubrey, who is still counting on me and looking to me for guidance and love, I must continue to honor what has gotten me to this point. Not only in this dreadfully sorrow filled situation but also in all other facets of my life.

As I sit and lament, there are three things that jump out immediately; **love, forgiveness & karma**.

Love and unconditional love in the case of the trial, I am referring to unconditional love and that means being better, not bitter. By allowing the bitterness and anger that I feel to pass through but not linger and destroy me.

This means releasing the emotions and the individual that has harmed me while understanding that I may now need to reassess, regroup and recalibrate my next choice in life.

In all other cases, love really is all you need. John Lennon was spot on. As much as my heart is breaking after losing Sydney, I know that my love for her and for life and for the rest of my family, love will get me through this. If I remain open hearted, allowing myself to feel through every stage of emotions this process presents, I will find a new strength. And what has been surfacing is a depth of love I have not dreamed possible and one that will continue to pull me through the dark moments that present themselves at the most unexpected times, then, now and in the future.

Forgiveness *is also non-negotiable and touches every aspect of life, every relationship and every choice. But in this case, as it relates to the trial, I want to continue to find a way to live* life with the lowest levels of stress and with a level of health that will afford me a long and healthy life (yes, I do still want this, knowing it may be a little longer till I see my Sydney again). As it relates to the defendant, I wish for him the ability to learn and grow from the consequences of the choices made on December 24th, 2016 and hope he finds peace and is able to change the course of the direction he has seemingly chosen to have sailed his ship of life (this gets me to karma). **Please understand forgiveness does not mean forgetting ...it means honoring my beautiful daughter and myself and dealing with the circumstances that we have been given. It is normal to want revenge, to allow hate in, inviting it to stay as a permanent resident, taking over all my responses, my every thought and my every day, and YES... I want him to serve a very long time, but I also know that the only things I can control are my responses (notice I did not say my reactions), my attitudes**

and adhering to my beliefs in honoring my beautiful daughter.

And last but not least, Karma...*no matter what the outcome, there is no bringing Sydney back to us in this lifetime. Whatever the decision comes to be, I do truly believe that karma will be served at some point whether in this lifetime, the next or perhaps the next, until the lesson is learned and the choices are changed...karma will indeed be served.*

I remember sitting and hearing somewhere in my mind the phrase, "karma is a bitch". As I was rereading my journal, I was reminded of a concept "to detach" from the end result or outcome. In doing so, I understand and accept that the outcome is out of my hands and my attachment to whatever takes place can only harm me if I allow it. This reminded me that I am at the mercy of the experts of the courts and for me to do anything other than find forgiveness for what transpires will only be to my own detriment. It doesn't hurt knowing both my girls are watching me to see how I handle this next step of the process and with each move there is a lesson to be learned. So, it was on that day that I created a 3-line mantra, which I frequently revisit, to help me stay focused and remind me during those more complicated moments of being human, to support the choice that I made on that day and every day following.

So, my reasons for wanting to write this book and sharing my story are really pretty simple, my two raisons d'etre, my daughters, because just like Sydney said..."*it is our love that fills, fuels and heals my next breath*". Sydney gave me the permission to not only live but to be extraordinary. My hope for you is through this book you are able to find your permission to live and to live extraordinary, in your time. Let's dive into the steps that are helping me do just that every day, starting with an overview of the process of grief itself.

Three – The Grief Wheel & Process

The Grief Wheel

Define New Reality

Shock, Anguish & Denial

Commemerative Tribute

Pain, Guilt, Anger & Regret

Service & Hope

Numb

Overwhelmed Sadness, Disbelief

Marcy STONE

The reason the grief wheel is a dream catcher is because it's purpose is very important to me and I hope you find it equally as meaningful. A dream catcher is believed to protect you from negative energy. People would hang one over their newborns crib so that all negative energy would flow through and away from the baby. All of the positive healing energy would flow down the strings in the center so all of the good energy would spill from the feathers into the baby's soul. This story gives me such peace, so it seems appropriate to utilize the dream catcher for our grief wheel. As we go through the process of feeling the pain and allowing ourselves to heal slowly and thoughtfully, the negative, hurtful emotions and thoughts go away and into the ethers. This allows all of the good that is still within and around us to flow down through the dream catcher onto the feathers and into our soul. This aids in our recovery, rediscovery and inviting peace and new beginnings.

The Grief Process

Starting this chapter with a visual seems appropriate because when you go online searching for "how to's" on the grief process and guidance through it, it all sounds so clean cut and organized and that is absolutely not the case. In fact, it is quite the opposite. So much comes into play about how you lived your life that helps mold and shape how you go through the horrific process of losing a child. How we lived while our baby was in our arms or holding our hands or waving to us as they leave the house, determines not only how we bounce around the stages of the grief process, especially the first 4 stages, but it also determines how we will punish ourselves, or not, through the process and add more grief and pain than is needed. This is a very human thing and one I hope I am able to help you negate as we move through the next few chapters together. The 3 final steps of the process, Service & Hope, Commemorative Tribute and Define New Reality, will be covered in more detail later in the book. Right now, we need to stay focused on the first 4 steps, without navigating them, the final 3 are not going to come from a place of peace and love, which will be critically important for you and your future, or as I call it, your new reality.

As far as I know, the grief process is one of the few processes that does not follow nice and neat arrows around in a clockwise flow. There is definitely no nice and neat and you do not experience any fluidity. If you follow the lines in the grief wheel, you may see what I mean. You will probably feel what it is depicting throughout this book. At any point in this journey of finding sanity and serenity, you will be bouncing from one point to another, depending on what you are experiencing at that moment in time. I found often I would go from anger and pain back to shock and anguish while still in anger and pain and so the loop continued. Staying present in each one of the steps was not hard initially. Staying present and not permanently staying in one or more of the steps of the process was something that needed to be monitored. This is one of the reasons why you will see me repeat "stay present" often through these next chapters. It is an important key to proactively and

The Voice of an Angel

mindfully find your way through the grief. I say proactive and mindful because while we naturally react in grief, we could stay in this horrific state for the rest of our lives if there is no proactive or mindfulness happening all during this roller coaster of emotions that grief invokes.

Taking a look back at the visual at the beginning of this chapter shows the stages of grief. They happen in any order that you are affected. The first two stages I was able to identify was *shock, anguish & denial* and *numb.* While they are self-explanatory by definition, it is important to understand that these steps are easy to get stuck on. If you aren't careful and don't stay present, you could unconsciously "choose" to stay in these 2 stages. Then oh my gosh...its game over. It is so very, easy to just want to stay here, but what you may not realize is that if you do choose to stay here, what you think you are avoiding, is exactly what you are doing to yourself. Allow me to explain. By unconsciously opting to stay in denial and numb you think you are not feeling and then time will pass and someday when you "wake up" you will feel better. That is absolutely not the case. It is the exact opposite. All you are doing is feeling more pain by staying in that state and prolonging the chance of ever truly feeling better. The same goes for stage 3, *pain, guilt, regret and anger.* This is another stage that can ultimately consume us if we aren't careful and don't have a plan on how to find some peace. The next is stage 4, *overwhelmed, sadness & disbelief.* This is also a place that could define us for the rest of our lives if we don't know how to move through it, releasing what hurts and finding ways to feel good again. Yes, it is very possible to feel good again.

The following chapters are designed to help you structure a healthy, solid foundation allowing you to move through these stages even though the movement is anything but fluid and neat.
For example, let's say the first three months you flux between, and sometimes all at once, shock, pain and anger and then you may branch out to

depression but then back again to pain. It can feel like a pinball machine of emotions, back and forth. I have found that this back and forth and back again, or the "pinball process" happens well into the second year of grief.

As you find yourself navigating the steps of the grief wheel by way of the pinball process, the following chapters will be extremely important, starting with understanding and embedding the basic fundamentals. How these fundamentals provide relief will be different for you then it was for me. I am sure they will help you navigate what could continually suck you into a black hole if not careful.

An example of NOT doing this was when I hit the one-year milestone. I was teetering in an upward turn and finding hope and all of a sudden, I became incredibly angry! **So very angry**! I have come to understand that because I was not numb and in shock like the prior December, I was able to experience anger in a way I hadn't before. In fact, I would almost call it rage. The emotions can be that extreme at times. I actually fought it for a time, and I did not remind myself of this process, which definitely made it worse. Instead of following this process, because I didn't want to feel like a pinball, I tried pushing the anger away. I only wanted to feel peace but the anger kept rising to the surface and I would explode! Not healthy at all and the opposite of how I handled the entire first year. I went back to the process, allowing the anger, but making sure it did not consume me by writing about how I felt and getting heavier into my physical activity. This provided an outlet for me to express frustration in a healthy way vs. holding it in or taking it out on the people I love. Once I was feeling a little more level headed, I reminded myself of forgiveness and how karma would have its day. That was the best way I could find to comfort myself at that time. I went back to this process many times.

I find it therapeutic to visualize the dream catcher and remind myself why I chose it to represent the process of grief. The dream catcher and its beautiful weaving allows me to release any negative thoughts and have them float away in the wind, taking away with them the pain and offering comfort in their place. Knowing that the hurt, the pain, the depth of the despair was already upon me, the feathers represent relief. This allows all my love to travel down the feathers and remember and embrace all of the good, the joy and the memories that help heal me over time. The scars will remain with me but knowing they are being healed with love and with my Angel's guidance and blessing, this is the gift I receive each time I look at the dream catcher.

Now we will dive into some basic fundamentals. If these have not been a part of your life before, I strongly urge you to take this next chapter very seriously. These fundamentals help promote balance in every day life so you can imagine the importance of them in this incredibly emotional and challenging time.

Grief Wheel — Shock, Anguish, Denial · Numb · Pain, Guilt, Anger & Regret · Overwhelmed, Sadness, Disbelief · Service & Hope · Commemorative Tribute · Define New Reality

Four – Basic Fundamentals

Throughout the next few chapters, my hope is to break things down in a way that you are able to relate with, and find ways to incorporate them in your life, and in a way that seemed helpful to me as I found my way. These basic suggestions can be helpful, both now as you go through this terrible repair of your heart and soul and then also later as you have found some peace and are more apt to seeing clearer. I know that feels impossible right now, so far from reach, but it does happen and I will be with you on your journey.

The following are what I believe to be basic fundamentals in every day normal life but, for where you are now in life, they are not basic, they are critical! These fundamentals need to be in place in order for you to find your way to create a healthy foundation so when the roller coaster of emotions occur, you have a solid base that won't crumble under you.

For example, Love, it's the first one I listed and that is intentional. We naturally love but we also instinctively want to stop loving when we get hurt or wounded. The items on the list that follow are vital steps to either start or revisit if you are already doing some of them. These items are suggestions that literally saved me from myself as I navigated this journey to my new reality.

Love - As much as your heart is breaking, during and after the loss of your beautiful baby, whether it's a sudden tragic accident or a slow painful illness, love is what will get you through it all. Love is powerful. It will behoove you to remain open hearted, allowing yourself to feel through every stage of emotions this process presents – its utilizing and moving with the love for the person you lost, that will help you move forward. It is a natural first instinct to shut down, get stuck or become bitter in all the things that now won't happen in life because the person you love is gone. This approach will only kill you slowly, each day to wake to another lifeless breath. Is that really what you think your beloved would want for you? It's amazing to me how often that statement has gotten me through so many tough moments then and even today.

Raison d'etre – my reason(s) for living. By now you have heard this term a few times and for me it is an essential element for my survival. I don't mean to sound dramatic but as you are unfortunately experiencing, it feels exactly like that, survival. This meant life or death for me and to this day, I remind AND THANK Aubrey, because she is my reason for living.

Voice of an Angel – not everyone is able to hear their Angel's voice and that is perfectly okay. Our children choose different ways to stay in touch with us once they are taken. Some communicate through feathers or pennies on the ground, some through music and some through signs. My Sydney does them all and if you ever met her, that makes perfect sense! So, if you haven't yet identified how you and your Angel will stay in touch, I happily share my messages and stories and that's exactly what Sydney wants me to do. Share, so you can find your way.

Staying Present – when Sydney came to me in a dream and said I needed to stay present in the pain, my initial reaction was "why in the world would I want to do that to myself?". But when she explained the reasons why, sadly it made sense and honestly as I did it, it wasn't as terrible as I thought, because I very naturally went right to my love for her and her sister. Perhaps it was because they saved my life before, many times, and now they were going to do it again as my raisons d'etre.

Now is a good time to better explain staying present with a simple, every day example, something I am positive everyone has experienced in his or her lifetime. Have you ever driven somewhere and when you arrive at your destination, you realized you missed most of the ride. And you were driving! Well this is the exact opposite of staying present.

By shutting down and living in the past you are more apt to suffer from depression. If you worry about the future and the what if's you are prone to suffer from anxiety. Both of these places are very easy to go to on a normal day, so you can imagine how you might go here under these circumstances. This is why Sydney was very clear about staying in the now, the present.

Sydney stated that by staying open to feeling the pain in all its varying degrees and stages allows your heart to stay open and allows the healing process to start immediately vs. waiting a year or so and then trying to figure out how to open your heart back up. Syd said, *"don't stop living momma, live through this. You will feel good again, I promise!"* So, she promised and so I stayed open.

How do you stay present? If you are crying tears of pain... cry, sob, share what's got you emotional in that moment, and be okay with it all. Who cares what anyone says or thinks! **Staying present, reminding yourself of your raison d'etre, feeling and listening to what you need; these 4 things flow hand in hand and will get you through all of the steps that follow.**

Slowing down and listening - Something to be mindful of now and moving forward is that your reality is changed. Well, actually it is now a new reality. And what does that mean? It will be different for each of us. By slowing down from what you used to do and listening to how you are reacting to things, emotionally, mentally and physically, you will discern what stays and what goes. Everything has changed for me. What mattered before may not matter now. What were your priorities then? Are they still in line with what you are feeling from your gut? Look at everything, especially over the first year: what is still needed, do you have the same interests, job satisfaction, family and friends, foods you used to eat, exercise routines, beliefs...everything! You are changing and unless you slow down, stay present and pay close attention to these things, you will find yourself more irritated, aggravated, short tempered and not exactly sure why. You will naturally attribute it to the grief you are experiencing from your incredible loss but grief is the trigger of all the change that follows. You can never be the person you were again, that chapter in life has ended. Now is the time to slowly discern who the new you will be. The key is slow and steady. No need to rush.

Someone you trust – THIS IS SO CRITICAL DURING THE INITIAL TIME OF LOSS and well into the first month(s) of your grieving process. When we are faced with the reality of having to plan a funeral, especially a loss that was completely unexpected, you need someone that can be your rock. Having a friend or family member that can be there in a moment's notice and be close and around for the foreseeable future is a very wise choice. Someone that you trust will have your best interest, and your lost loved one, at heart when any decision or detail is determined. I say this because from the time you are informed of the loss of your loved one, to a few weeks after the funeral, you are not in your right mind, let alone in the right frame of mind to think of things like pictures and music to play and who to notify and where to hold the funeral. This person is not only going to help make it all happen but they will also be able to remind you of what happened and how, weeks after the fact, when you wonder about certain details and questions. They can also assist with finding professionals like legal counsel or accountants, if necessary.

As the reality of your loss sets in, so does the other stuff associated with it, both before that moment and following. This person will also need to be sure that you don't sign anything during this time period!! At least not without them or someone else looking it over first. This is for your safety. This even includes the funeral arrangements. Having a fresh and stable set of eyes protecting you is crucial at this time in your life.

Overall wellbeing – right now the phrase "overall wellbeing" probably prompts a lackluster reaction and I am completely sympathetic and feel your pain. It is, however, **incredibly paramount** to what we are trying to do together. This is a large part of how you can stay in touch and open to the pain. Sounds like gluten for punishment, I know. Remember, the premise behind staying open to feeling the pain is allowing your heart to stay open and heal so that you will again, be able to get back into a life that feels and makes some sense. This is possible and so it's important to take care of ALL of you.

Let's start with a few wellbeing items that are easy to obtain and you will feel some immediate relief as you get into the other, more basic lifestyle adjustments. The physical body will react and recover differently than your emotional or mental body so you need to address each of them through this process.

Please do what you can to avoid becoming medicated, in any fashion. I believe that to be completely detrimental to the overall healing process. Becoming "numb" is not going to help you, ever!

Breathe – this is something I never thought I would have to be reminded to do but from the second I heard that Sydney was gone I seem to hold my breath. I am much more mindful of it now but it still happens and seems like I freeze with tension, stress and when I'm not staying present. It certainly is an interesting reminder to stay present. What works for me is when I notice I am doing this, I take a deep full belly breath and hold it for a count of 5 then slowly exhale. This provides me the opportunity to stop, regroup and come back to focus. It also helps diminish the stress or at least make it manageable vs. having that lurking feeling of panic set in.

Stress – if you are anything like me, I show my stress in my face, specifically my eyes. I found using a simple lavender eye pillow every day when I was resting, gave me some relief both internally and externally. A great website for an eye pillow and other natural healing remedies is www.thrivemarket.com and they have a wonderful selection of items for stress, relaxation and overall wellbeing.

B Complex Stress Support – I don't claim to be a doctor, however, multiple people suggested this to me from the medical profession as well as the homeopathic arena. I found it to be very helpful, B complex aids in supporting the emotional & psychological wellbeing. Many people fall into a state of depression after the tragic loss of a child and I can absolutely see how that is possible. Your world, as you know it, has been totally destroyed. Taking a B Complex can aid you, along with the other things suggested throughout this chapter and this book. I am fortunate enough to have a reliable, knowledgeable holistic apothecary shop near me but this natural supplement can also be found at www.thrivemarket.com. Here is one of so many websites out there to learn more... www.wellnessmama.com.

Stay or get physically active – walking or keeping your fitness routine is a powerful tool through the process of realizing your loss AND aiding with any anxiety associated with it as well as adapting to your new reality. Physical activity is also an excellent way to deal with stress as it channels the energy into something functional and positive.

Nutrition – first thing here is to make sure you are eating!! No matter what your normal relationship is with food, the initial stages of grief seem to want to remove food from the equation. While it may be great for an initial 6-pound loss, it can affect you in detrimental ways after the initial first ten or so days pass. Depletion of nutrients can send your body into a number of different, unhappy and unhealthy directions. So, when that person you trust is saying, "you need to eat something", listen to them, please!! Start small, but eat. This is where we go back to listening again. Your body will tell you what it needs to remain healthy to support you, including your emotional needs. If you are craving a piece of fish, eat a piece of fish. There is a very high probability that the foods that you loved before, may no longer serve you. So, it will be really important for you to stay present and listen.

Specialists – another important element to staying present and listening to what you need is finding someone or something that aids in your process of addressing natural healing. Again, please do your best not to medicate.

A counselor, grief counselor or even a spiritual grief counselor - can be extremely beneficial. There comes a time when that person(s) that has been there for you from the beginning is not only going to need to get back into their own life but they are also out of their league as it relates to supporting your journey into this new reality from a deep emotional level. Finding someone you can share your raw and tattered emotions with, and is able to provide you with some comfort and counsel can help keep you moving forward in healthy ways.

Acupuncture - Signs of imbalance will show in the body and Acupuncture can be of incredible help to those suffering from grief or sadness immediately after a loss and can help relieve the struggles to "move on." Chinese medicine aligns the meridians, balancing the Qi, or energy, in both the emotional and physical body. You can begin to feel more grounded and better able to cope with the loss. Whether or not you understand the science behind it and even if you tend to doubt the possibilities of it working, what else do you have to lose?

Chinese Organ Body Clock – I am sharing this because as I have experienced with my own loss and also with clients I have worked with, interrupted sleep is a natural side effect of grief. After doing the research and proving its accuracy, it feels necessary to include it here for you. There is much more information for each time shared below, as well as for the rest of the day so I included the link below if you would like to peruse at a deeper level. It truly is a remarkable science. What I have included is what wakes you, associated with grief. If you find you wake up often between certain times, the information below can give you a starting point on where you might want to do some deeper internal diving of what you need to bring to the surface, to be present, so you are able to move past it and get a good nights sleep. I have needed to revisit this often and found it to be very helpful.

*Information from www.foreverconscious.com.

9-11pm Feelings of paranoia or confusion may be felt.

11pm-1am Subconscious feelings of resentment may appear during this time.

1-3am This is also the time of anger, frustration and rage.

3-5am This time is associated with feelings of grief and sadness.

5 am to 7 am At this time, emotions of defensiveness or feelings of being stuck could be evoked.

No regrets! - Not to sound harsh or rash during this time of mourning but while feeling regret is normal for us as humans, it is something that stems from society. If we don't appear to have some regret in losing a child then we are a monster! There is a difference between regretting and grieving. Regret is "I wish I would have..." and that is pointless and serves no healthy purpose and certainly not something your baby wants you to lament. What's past is unchangeable. It's a natural human thing to wonder all the usual "what ifs" but it is really counter intuitive. Deep down you know this, but we always seem to want to "own" vs. "accept" what is.

If you can allow yourself to honor the life that you and your sweet child had together, knowing you did your best and loved them with every ounce of your being, then you have the permission to wash away the urge to fall into regret. This is a useless punishment and if people judge you for taking a healthy outlook to how you are approaching this stage of the process, they may not be someone you need to have in your new reality.

Being honest with yourself – this is something I have watched my clients struggle with throughout their grief process. There are many reasons why and all are personalized by the relationships they had with their children. If

I may share something, that while it sounds simple enough to do; sometimes there is a struggle with the execution of it in life and love. There is a small difference between honest and kindness. When you tell a little white lie to protect the feelings of someone you love on what you believe to be a little or unimportant matter, this is still being dishonest. It is possible to find a kind way to be completely honest with someone that avoids the little white lie and allows you to remain true to yourself. Unfortunately, this is something that not many people do.

At this critical time in your life, it is so incredibly important that you practice this level of honesty but first with yourself and the world around you. If there is something that is happening that does not feel right or good to you as you are going through this process of grief, stop immediately!! Stop and change it, no matter what it is! This is not the time to humor others, rationalize or try to keep the peace, not within you or with others. If something feels bad, do what you can to change it and do your best to be kind about it. We will touch on this more later, but please stop for a moment and think about where you are in your healing, how others want you to heal vs. what would feel right, good or best for you.

By mindfully addressing and incorporating each of these fundamentals, I hope that you can find some peace within these steps as you move through your days. Surviving the loss of a child is not something everyone is able to help you navigate and grief is so very personal and unique for each of us. My wish for you is to find some solace in knowing you are not alone. I know you are questioning how you are going to survive and what will my life look like now, how am I ever going to move forward and even do I want to survive!

Those questions and others were what I asked. What you will find in the following chapters are the answers I was given to help myself and now, I hope to help you through this devastating time.

Let's do a quick recap of the basic fundamentals
so you are able to reflect back with one snapshot;

- ♥ Love
- ♥ Raison d'etre
- ♥ Voice of an Angel
- ♥ Staying present
- ♥ Slowing down and listening
- ♥ Someone you trust
- ♥ Overall wellbeing
- ♥ No regrets
- ♥ Be honest with yourself

Remember to check out all of the resources listed
throughout this chapter to support you as
naturally as possible and to keep you healthy
during the most challenging time in your life.
Trust me when I say, there will be a moment in
the future where you will "come to" and wish
someone told you to do what you can to take care
of yourself, even if it is only the basic
fundamentals. I will be that person, right now,

telling you! These will be lifesavers a few months down the road, please take heed.

Now, we will begin to tie in what I refer to as "Core Values" which can help shape your world and provide direction on how to treat yourself and one another. By consistently living the basic fundamentals and tying in the next chapter of Core Values, you will slowly begin to feel a new foundation forming. This will replace the one that has been forever lost and will no longer serve you in this next phase of your life, the developing of your new reality.

Basic Fundamentals	Love	Voice of an Angel	Slow Down & Listen	Overall Wellbeing	No Regrets
	Raison d'être	Staying Present	Someone You Trust	Be Honest With Yourself	

Five - Core Values

A Core Value basically means what we expect from each other and ourselves.

Journal entry - 365 days...or 8,760 hours...or 525,600 minutes...

How has one year come to pass? It feels like only yesterday receiving the news, going to the morgue, planning the funeral. Getting dressed for the funeral I recall looking into the mirror and not recognizing the face that looked back at me. It wasn't until later that I realized what that signified and then found myself on a journey of self rediscovery while also dealing with this indescribable loss. I was blessed with a few visits from my beloved Sydney in my dreams over this year and she has taken me places, showed me things, shared insights of why now, who I am becoming and why I need to be strong and find my way and, with no surprise, she promised me she would always be by my side, like she was in life...my side kick, but with more of a reach to help than when she was here.

Her selflessness and her simplicity in life was so beautiful and it got me to thinking of how we could honor her today. She had so many ways of living that if more people followed suit, the world would be a much happier place. So I thought I would share some of her "Syd'ism's or ways to live life". Some were so simple, silly and some were wisdom beyond her years, core values of a pure, simple soul...

So here we go...

1. *Dr. Seuss rocks. Two of her favorites (she had them posted in her room), <u>"Today you are you! That is truer than true! There is no one alive who is you-er than you!"</u> And... <u>"Be who you are and say what you feel, because those who mind don't matter and those who matter don't mind".</u>*
2. *SLOW DOWN!!!! And be home more.*
3. *Give the person you are with 100% of your attention, let them know they matter.*
4. *Family is everything! (this is everyone that matters to you, not just blood!).*
5. *Love really is the only thing that matters, all kinds of love.*
6. *Never say diet. Eat in moderation, except with bacon!!!*
7. *Don't take life, or yourself, too seriously.*

8. NEVER change who you are for someone else.
9. Love with reckless abandon.
10. Give all you have and expect nothing in return.
11. Live life so you will have zero regrets.
12. Material stuff DOES NOT MATTER!
13. There is always room for 2nds; 2nd breakfast, 2nd lunch and 2nd dinner (she was a foodie!).
14. Pooh "You're braver than you believe, stronger than you seem, and smarter than you think.
15. Only be around people that believe in you.
16. Why lie when the truth is so much fun
17. Only have a bucket list if you intend on using it!
18. Choose the people in your life by their heart.
19. The most important ingredient in a recipe is the love you put into it.
20. Never ask someone to do something you wouldn't do, and if you wouldn't do it, does it even really truly matter?
21. Don't cry because it's over. Smile because it happened. (More profound words from Dr. Seuss).

I know we all miss her so dreadfully and to see people posting their feelings and pictures today is such a testament to what an incredibly loving soul Sydney was and is. I would like to ask everyone to light a candle in her honor today. I found a two-wick candle in a beautiful mercury glass; the one wick signifies her 21 beautiful years with us in this lifetime and the other wick signifies her beautiful soul as she now watches over each and every one of us. Let her continue to share her wisdom with us all in new ways. Watch and listen for her, she is with us all, which I believe brings her great joy and it brings me a sense of peace and a knowing that I am never alone.

During our lifetime together, the girls and I lived by a few very powerful Core Values. We felt they were important to not only be wonderful individuals but these values also kept us growing together over the years, making our "we 3" relationship stronger as the years passed. Never underestimate your children's understanding or intelligence. We were having these conversations well before the girls' teenage years. In reading Syd's list of 'isms, it tells you just how wise children are. By asking them to help create how we were going to live an extraordinary life, it provided them with ownership and a clear understanding of choice and consequence.

Not completely understanding the term "Core Value" at that age but understanding the concept of how they would enhance our lives, the girls openly embraced them after the divorce. We all adapt and incorporate ideals relating to our moral compass differently.

After my divorce and we became "we 3", there were some hard moments for the girls. They would wonder what they did wrong, why did daddy leave and as time passed, they would grow angry. So, I created a safe space for them in our garage, a graffiti wall. They were allowed to use spray paint, (what kid doesn't want to be able to paint on a wall in their home!) and express their emotions, no matter what they were. The only catch was for every negative or angry emotion they needed to also paint something good, positive or loving. Over the years, this was such an excellent parenting tool, even more than I initially guessed, because it allowed me to see where they were in their heads and hearts which enabled me to sooth, guide, comfort and love them exactly how they needed to be loved. It was also a subliminal way to continue to promote the Core Values that helped us shape our lives together in beautiful ways.

As they grew up, they both had their own way of expressing what they learned, but it was very clear to me that these values embedded their way into the girls' way of being. As their momma bear, this made me incredibly proud of them.

Core Values can help shape your world in altruistic and benevolent ways. Core Values provide direction on how to treat one another. By consistently living the Core Values provided in this chapter, along with the Guiding Principles and the Basic Fundamentals in the prior chapters, you will experience outstanding outcomes.

After Sydney was taken from me, I knew that while the Core Values we established were a fabulous way to raise us as a family, they were going to absolutely support me in the deep dig I needed to do to find my way through the grief, especially the initial shock and anguish I was experiencing. There was a time when I was surprised that I was able to find the next breath, that's how devastating this is to a momma bear. But you already know that feeling, don't you?

I was left in a place of darkness knowing I needed to find even a small ray of light in order to figure out how I was going to do this thing called life. Then I heard it again, that sweet voice, *"momma, feel the pain. Lean into it. Let the love heal you"*. **Love.** That's what she was trying to tell me, guide me. She knows I will be looking for how to survive this and she remembers how we lived and the conversations we had deciding on the path together. Sydney is telling me that the first step or Core Value in grief is Love. So, love is what I did, from that moment on. I used all the love I had within my entire being to muscle the next logical thought (and all of this processing happened within a nano-second!) because in that moment, my oldest daughter is walking through my front door, sobbing asking me to please tell me this is all some dreadful mistake and Sydney is still alive. Love. Sobbing, I hugged her hard and just cried with her. There were no words for this moment, only love, and I gave her all that I had.

When Sydney was younger, she bought me a book, "I love you more". That was the beginning of what became one of my "favoritist" things ever! From that moment on, "I love you more" was a thing we did. Every day, it was a race to see who could beat the other. She was tricky and always setting me up, and I loved it. She would leave notes in my lunch (role reversal!) and I would leave notes on her pillow or bathroom mirror and sometimes on a treat I would get her from the grocery store. We were not shy about sharing our love or about saying it.

When her big sister bought a house, one of the first things she and her husband did was invite Sydney over to ask her what color she wanted "her room". She was beyond thrilled at this!! They were so close, even though Aubrey had moved on to the next stage of her life and they both worked full time, they found ways to stay "together". It was beautiful to watch and honestly a bit of an arm pincher for me to see, I mean, it's what every momma bear wants for her girls, to remain close and show their love for each other. The girls knew how to say and show "I love you more" in actions as well as words.

The next Core Value came to me as quickly and almost directly after Love did and it is **Compassion**. Through the initial moments I realized I had compassion for that poor police officer that had to deliver this horrifying news. I had compassion for the family of the man responsible for this irreversible loss and I even had compassion for him as he lay in a coma fighting for his life.

Compassion takes the love and allows it to broaden its spectrum of coverage, so to speak. Allowing an unconditional love to flow their way, perhaps aiding in whatever peace they might need in this moment. Compassion is the antithesis of wishing death to the man that took Sydney's trust for granted and at that moment that could have been incredibly easy to do. That, however, would not bode well for my karma and I am a believer in karma. I don't believe it is possible to make Karma a core value. It is a result of our thoughts and actions, the concept or result of what his or my karma would be. This is what initially helped me find compassion and has continued to be a driving force for me through this journey.

Patience...this has always been one of my least favorite words. It is something that throughout my life I have needed to be extra mindful of, not patience with others but with myself. I can find patience all day long for another person and perhaps this is part of what makes me good at what I do for a living. But when it comes to being patient with myself, I would get a big fat "D" as a grade. So, patience is absolutely on this list of core values in surviving this loss that still feels so surreal to me.

In knowing my less than kind approach to myself in the area of patience, I choose to continue to work and help people throughout the course of my first year of grieving. In looking back, I feel it has been instrumental to my sanity. This is why I promote service throughout the grief process and why there is a "Service" step in the grief wheel. When my work would slow down through the first year, I found other ways to be of service to help me find patience. This is a reason service came to be in my process.

I have always been incredibly hard on myself, expecting amazing outcomes in, I've been told, unrealistic timelines. However I expect nothing from others, only what they are able to do and in their own time. So, by helping others, I was able to see their grief or pain and for whatever reason, it provided me with a brief permission to be patient with myself, because I, too, am suffering. Now, I never said this was logical, normal or even sane, but I believe it to be partly why I can do what I do in life. The key is understanding myself well enough and making the necessary adjustments. The more people I can be there for and help, allows me to heal. It's an interesting twist to the Wounded Healer Archetype.

Honesty is the next critical player in the line up of Core Values to survive grief. For me, being honest with myself, about my lack of patience for myself gave me the ability to find a way out vs. pretending and eventually falling into the forever abyss of misery.

Being honest with yourself can sometimes be hard even on a normal day. To find complete honesty, no white lies or rationalizing, within your crushed and broken heart can be a challenge. We sometimes want to own what took place vs. allowing and being real about it. We did the best we could as momma bears at every stage in their sweet lives. We need to let them spread their wings accordingly. There comes a time when we need to allow them to be responsible for their own choices. That statement right there, for me, would be an incredibly easy one to be dishonest with myself.

As a momma bear, I could own Sydney's choice to trust that man with the consequence being her precious life. I could "own" that choice, finding all sorts of ways to torture myself and say things like "if I only" but what would be the point? I raised my daughter to trust her gut with an open mind until she got a solid read of him. She unfortunately did not have the opportunity to complete her due diligence. He proved her wrong. Do you see how, as a momma bear, I could own that responsibility? In doing so, I would never find any peace and be silently tortured for the remainder of my life.

The choice to be honest with myself is not only saving my life but it is also how I raised my girls to be. If either of them found me not abiding by one of our Core Values, there would be hell to pay, especially under these circumstances. The expression, "life is short" is truer than most people realize but you and I both sadly understand. You have a choice here, being honest with yourself, no matter how hard it can be, can be a key element to surviving the grief wheel.

By now you will have seen this next concept throughout the first few chapters and I assure you that this will not be the last: **Forgiveness**. If you remember in the beginning of the book I mention, "love, forgiveness, karma", it's not a surprise that Love and Forgiveness would be the bookends of our warrior core values either. Both are incredibly powerful and absolutely necessary pieces to this journey.

Have you ever seen someone that holds grudges? How they have a darkness about them and seem to age faster and express animosity towards mostly everyone they encounter? Not fun people to be around, are they? Without love or forgiveness, this is exactly how you will end up! I don't want this for you, it's no way to live and especially if you want to live a good life again and do things to honor your sweet baby. So how do you find forgiveness then? It starts with love. You knew I was going to say that, didn't you? Love really is the key to everything. I am not sure I can explain this clearly without another example from my journal:

January 29, 2017 - Being completely vulnerable, Sundays are probably one of the harder days for me as a momma and friend, missing my Sydney. It was our "snuggle & pink blankie pj veg day". Sometimes we had hours and sometimes only an hour but it was always quality and treasured.

As we were cleaning up the Christmas stuff this year, I found the perfectly wrapped present Sydney had left for me and in my favorite leopard print paper, no less. I hesitated opening it, but did and in it was just another reminder of just how special she was and how well she knew me and valued our special moments. In the package was a cozy shirt that says "Sundays are for snuggling"...

So today is Sunday and I find myself ebbing a bit, but am being kind to myself, allowing the emotions and staying with the goodness of the memories and feeling the love that flows through my veins. I am still not ready to wear that shirt and it needs to last me for the rest of my life.

Can you feel the love in that entry? It is the depth of that all-encompassing love that allows me to find forgiveness within my being and in doing so, over the long term, I save myself from becoming that retched, grudge holding curmudgeon. Embracing love allows me to help others find that same level of love within them to heal and find compassion. This means forgiving yourself as well as someone else.

You are still wondering how, aren't you? Forgiveness can be a tough lesson and as we continue through the chapters, you will be guided through how to allow forgiveness to permeate your entire being. The steps of the 6 A's will show you how to release what no longer serves and what is detrimental to you, which are necessary steps to finding and experiencing forgiveness. It is imperative that you understand, embrace and allow, in order to move through a healthier process in preparation for what could come next. I say "could" because it all depends on you and your level of will and determination and, yes, love.

Core Values

♥ Love

♥ Compassion

♥ Patience

♥ Honesty

♥ Forgiveness

You should have a general understanding of how and why I came up with these Core Values. Using the spiral graphic below, starting directly in the center at that dreadful moment of loss, when everything feels like it has completely shut down and you can't breath, feel or comprehend, you have entered a black hole and everything around you is dark and cold. That is what the center of this graphic depicts. If you are anything like me, this is probably how you felt for a period of time. When you are in that black hole of despair, it is vital that you feel all the love you have within you and lean into it. By doing so, you are enabling your heart to remain open and this is how you will survive, and in time, thrive. By following the spiral, understanding you will pinball back and forth, use it as a lifeline.

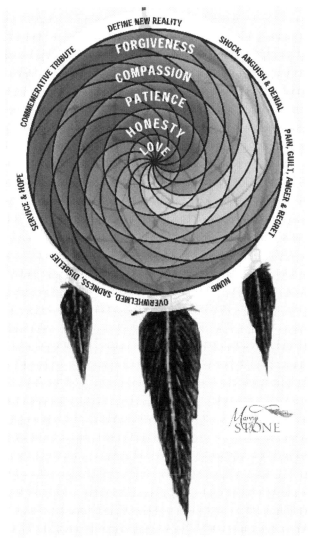

You will travel through the stages of the grief wheel by utilizing the spiral of Core Values to help keep you focused and grounded on what is best for you and a reminder of the direction your raison d'etre and your Angel would want you to travel.

Core Values	Compassion	Patience	Love	Honesty	Forgiveness

Six – Guiding Principles

As I was going through the first few months after losing my daughter, I was guided to stay very attentive to what I was feeling, I was also being guided on ways of dealing with all that was coming at me. I often felt like I was in a hailstorm being pummeled by huge pieces of ice with no relief or end in sight. As I was surviving each storm, I would journal what was happening and the concepts that seemed to be making an impact with me, because I knew I would be writing this at some point and wanted to make sure you had everything I could give you. My business mind kicked in often, which was a saving grace, because it reminded me how to separate the emotion from the task at hand. I'm sure that sounds harsh but there were times when it absolutely provided a moment of relief, as I navigated this grief process.

Thanks to my business hat, I was able to find ways of categorizing what helped me through that dark tunnel. The first level of this foundational process is the "basic fundamentals" that are explained in Chapter 4. The things that you will need to embrace on a daily basis to take care of you, benefiting you long after you find the light at the end of the tunnel. Some are ones, that before this tragedy, you wouldn't have needed, but going forward, you will be grateful for. As those fundamentals become your foundation, and you are now mindful of the Core Values and finding ways or checkpoints to assure you are staying present, you are ready for the next piece of the grief puzzle.

With that said, next is a list that we will refer to as "Guiding Principles". In business, guiding principles are for decision making and when consistently applied, aid in ensuring you stay on track in meeting your goals. The list of guiding principles that I have created, along with living the basic fundamentals, were instrumental in my ability to move forward in the healthiest way I saw possible while still dodging the pummeling from the hailstorms. The following chapters will provide more detail but for now, let's explore this list.

- ♥ Identify your raison d'etre
- ♥ Staying present
- ♥ Feeling the pain
- ♥ Leaning into the love you feel
- ♥ You still have to matter
- ♥ Listening to your gut
- ♥ Be vulnerable
- ♥ Share to heal
- ♥ Detachment

As I mentioned, this list grew over time into what I have come to believe to be critical through this process, and some of the things I realized I was already doing prior to the loss of my daughter. The difference now vs. then is the outcomes now are very different than they were then. Through reevaluating what each of these bullets means and how to allow them to mold you into "the new you" and your "new reality", is all a part of this journey through grief.

Can becoming a "new you" be avoided? Many people that I have worked with, after they have lost a precious child, have asked me that very question. The answer I provide them is that you are not meant to stay the same through life. We are meant to grow and shape and reshape with each lesson and experience we have. That is no different in the unfortunate experience of losing a child. The conscious difference is that we have the choice to make it either a manageable and eventual new reality with love, forgiveness and hope or we can find our way to perpetual misery, sorrow and soulful emptiness. These choices are yours to make and over the course of this book you are provided with ideas, suggestions and concepts that may challenge this very decision. Utilize the bullets above for good, for finding your way through the darkness into your light, however you design it to shine or sparkle.

How do you begin that journey?

Your raison d'etre. Your "other reason" for living, is the one that still walks beside you on this earth. I mention this and will continue to do so. I cannot stress the value and magnitude of importance of this one item. Who looks to you for guidance, comfort and love? You are needed on this earth! Please **stay present**! Show the people that love you that even in the darkest moments in your life, that you can be there for them AND do what you need for you. This is a delicate balance and one that needs to be nurtured for the rest of your life. You matter AND you need to be strong. A tough thing to say and ask of someone that just lost a child, I know. I am sorry but I know you have it within you. You are a warrior and have survived much in the course of your life already. You can and will survive this. I promise.

Feel the pain! Share and show your emotions, allow the people in your world to see you emote, this is strength. Be vulnerable, **lean into the love**, allow every emotion and share what is in your heart so those around you feel you. Know its okay for them to be exactly where they are, then show them how to find the strength of the love that permeates within your entire vessel. Allow this love to help you take your first step and then the next.

The people that love you and look to you need to see what you will do so they can be guided. You wear the hat of the matriarch. Be the queen of your kingdom in ways never before! The queen grieves and shares so that her people see her human side, her vulnerability, but then finds the strength to pull it together because she knows the people look to her. The queen is a warrior displaying elegance, compassion, courage and strength. That queen warrior energy is within you, that's why you chose this book. You do things differently than most or you have the capacity to do things differently. Up until now you played it safe and conformed some to fit into society. Well there is no more of that. Your time has come to put on that crown, or headdress and be that person you are meant to be. It is a sad thing that sometimes it takes our greatest loss or tragedy to bring out what has been lying dormant within us.

I believe it's important to mention here that I am not saying to become the martyr and put yourself and your needs on the back burner. Quite the contrary! *I am asking you to honor all that you are, be as honest with yourself and others as humanly possible in all capacities and live by example.*

Your List

That was a mouthful, wasn't it? And at all times, now with such a devastating loss!! Well, I'll let you in on a little secret...now is when you can get away with a few things; you are expected to act a little crazy and do potentially outlandish things because we are "not in our right minds". Use that to your favor. Yes, I am serious! Focus your energy, identifying what no longer works for you in your life; relationships, material possessions, jobs, your personal style, even where you live. Make a list (link to template in final chapter) of all of these things and how they used to serve you well but now no longer feel like you. You will see and feel subtle adjustments within your being, so this list is going to be very important to you over the next few months.

This list, while initially it's only a piece of paper, is going to help you reshape you and your life over time. It will help you start to feel again and feel better about who you are, what direction you are now going and who will be by your side as you move forward. Sounds a little crazy, I am sure, but trust me when I say that each month as you move through this grief process you are going to see and feel new and different. Part of the next stage of your process is being okay with all of that. What you do with this list will depend on how well you harness the balance of the queen or warrior energy within you. It is extremely important that you hold and build the list for a few months before taking any action. Action too soon could cause regret later and we do not want that.

Okay, so the list is being created with notations of what goes, stays, needs to be added, and what to hold, to simply monitor for a time.

There is something else that we as humans seem to do. We tend to want to own vs. allow. Owning something... meaning stopping the very progress of its healing vs. allowing and honoring the feelings to flow through us, continuing to move forward without concerning ourselves with speed.

Owning only promotes an added layer of grief that we certainly don't need or deserve but unfortunately people seem to like to take responsibility for things that really don't make any sense. To own the consequence of someone else's choice is illogical and is the behavior of a martyr. We are steering all of our energy and focus away from anything resembling martyr energy. It is completely counterproductive and most definitely not something your Angel above would want for you. If you find yourself headed in this direction, it's okay. **By your staying present you are able to catch this detrimental action and by demonstrating patience and going back to finding the love you are leaning on, you will navigate back to a more positive and less self-punishing mindset.**

There is absolutely no need for punishment. Replace punishment with patience. Patience for ourselves during this incredibly difficult time is paramount. Punishment is another unnecessary yet very normal thing I watch people do during their grieving process. No matter what the circumstances, you are not responsible for someone else's choice and whatever may have happened during your life together does not warrant punishment now. Harsh as this may sound, it is pointless and certainly isn't going to help you survive this process in any healthy sort of way and it isn't bringing your sweet love back. If you find yourself there, go back through the bullets and the highlights above, do some journaling, talk with your counselor, schedule an acupuncture appointment and refocus on finding the good in this journey. There is good in every journey, it is up to us to look for it and embrace it. My journey will always look different than yours and being okay with where you are in your timeline of your process is an important part of this puzzle.

We are alike in only one way; we both lost our precious bundle of joy. In all other ways, we are unique. As I continue to share my learning's through my loss, my goal is that you are able to find your unique way of incorporating the steps as they make sense and feel right to you. Your "cake" will turn out very different than mine but it will still be beautiful, robust and as individual as you.

Remaining beautiful and robust must be hard to wrap your head around right now. I mean, I remember not feeling beautiful and least of all robust during the first year of my loss. I was anything but these things and the thought of ever being them again was not in my sight, near or far. But I was incredibly fortunate enough to have the visits from my Angel to guide me and promise me that it was not only possible but also probable. I only had to do as she requested, which is all of what I am sharing with you in this book. So...I did. *"I mattered"*, she told me. *"Momma, **you still have to matter"**.

Well my first reaction to that was, honestly, ugh...seriously? There were moments where I thought this book should be titled, "slapped by an Angel" because it was during this time that Sydney was hard on me and rightly so. I was feeling sorry for myself, and while I had my raison d'etre, I still wasn't completely 'bought in" on the entire plan she was laying out for me. I was still trying to remember how to inhale and exhale. However, I listened to my Angel and told myself I still matter.

Now most thought I was crazy when I walked into my usual Saturday morning step class at the gym the Saturday after the funeral. The room went silent as soon as they saw me. Then the whispers started and I can only imagine what they were saying. It was then that my little group hugged me and encouraged me on because I immediately doubted my choice to **listen to my gut**, which means in part, taking care of my vessel as that helped stabilize my mental state. Society would tell me that I was crazy to be "out and about" already, let alone working out, but I listened to what I knew I needed for me, because I still mattered and that meant taking care of myself, partly for me but also for my raison d'etre.

After class was over, I was extremely grateful that I went and it felt good when people came over to me and hugged me and expressed their condolences. As humans, we instinctively think that "whispering" is bad, come to find out with each hug, it was quite the opposite. I also realized that day that it felt good knowing that I mattered and my daughters mattered to others too, and for a moment I didn't feel as alone. I am not normally one that looks externally for validation or approval but that day, I was grateful to have experienced the external love from my friends. I share that because we forget that while we are strong and independent women, there are times that if we listen to our gut and we allow ourselves to **be vulnerable**, people do the same thing right back to you in return. It is a beautiful exchange and unfortunately not one many experience, because we are always so on guard. *Grief has taught me vulnerability for sure.*

In sharing my story, so many people have been brave and reached out to me to share theirs. Sharing can really help the healing process. Think about this for a moment. We have so much love in our hearts and it pours out for all of those amazing people in our lives. Now we have this black hole in our heart and soul that was our beloved and we can no longer express our love for them the way we once did. So, we overflow with what I now call a 'grief cocktail'. It is all of the love we have with no place we would really want to direct it anymore, added to all of the other emotions that can often overtake us in an instant and it numbs us. If however we **share to heal**, we are going to experience a win-win.

By our being vulnerable and sharing what we are experiencing, in a way that promotes the opportunity of stimulating positive emotions for healing, then we are helping others. People that may have had a similar loss are also gaining things like; not feeling alone, feeling a strength stir within them that was lost, finding a smile that may have been eluding them for some time and even simply the chance to share their pain. Sharing pain and getting it out, even for a moment, provides space inside for some goodness that can help you move through the times of weakness or a low moment.

Sharing to heal has also helped a great deal in harnessing the capacity of finding forgiveness. No matter what the circumstances, forgiveness can be a tough dish to serve. Sometimes this means forgiving ourselves. There are other times such as awaiting the court date for the criminal trial or finding a place for the individual that took Sydney's trust for granted that cost her sweet life. I do recall covering forgiveness in the prior chapter but, like in life, it is something that requires multiple visitations, situation by situation. If you are anything like me, you realize that without embracing forgiveness, you, your life, health and happiness are in grave danger.

It does not matter how much you might dislike or even hate someone, but your judgment of them, which is one of my least favorite words or behaviors on the planet, serves no purpose and has no satisfactory end result. As sad as it is and as hard as it is to hear (and say), there is nothing that can ever happen that will bring our baby's back to us. That is something, believe it or not, through this process of grief, you can come to terms with in a healthy and guilt free way. Finding forgiveness in your heart and soul is what allows you to start to find some peace.

It is normal, despite what society and others may think as appropriate, to want to be happy again. The first step to that is being okay with wanting to be happy again. People; family, friends, co-workers, neighbors, transfer the way they "think" they would grieve if they lost a child (this is after they thank God that it didn't happen to them) and then from that point on, anything we do "our way" for our own sanity and needs is wrong, in their eyes. My first reaction was, and still is, "screw them" but that's not very politically correct, so I found a nicer way to express it, listening to your gut.

There is absolutely nothing wrong in wanting to be happy and you can want this at any time in your grieving process. So, if you start feeling this way three months after the loss of your beloved, then that is healthy for you and honor it. Will you stray from this feeling from time to time? Absolutely!

People will always be people and they will always have opinions. They will assume things about you and that is their choice. You have a choice to not allow their "ways" to alter your journey. The list you are still compiling of all of the things that are changing. Perhaps, some of these people will find themselves on the "no longer serves" list and they will be gone eventually anyway.

You have the absolute right to decide going forward you are going to dye your hair purple and blue and then not worry about what anyone thinks. Decisions and choices are going to be a very, very large part of this journey and please don't let someone that has not walked in your shoes tell you otherwise. Most people will tell you not to make any big decisions during the first year or so of grief. I would say listen to your gut. That is the reason for the list I asked you to start to create in the earlier part of this chapter. By creating this list, you are monitoring all of the things that no longer feel right. Tracking those changes, so that when you are stronger and feeling a little more like taking on the world (because sometimes that's exactly what it feels like), you have the confidence in your direction because you have done the work (the list). Having the list also provides something you can have control over, which can produce a small amount of peace during this time.

You have been staying present, feeling the pain and what it has been changing within you and that brings us to listening to your gut. Always remember that no matter what you do you can always change it again. Everything can be temporary vs. permanent and in looking at it that way, you may feel less stress in making a decision or a choice. When I came to realize that the only thing in this process that is permanent is the reason why I am in this process in the first place, I found some peace in that and relaxed a bit on the uncertainties that lie before me.

As you are detaching from some of your old ways from the list you have created, there is another form of **detachment** I would like to bring to your awareness. Detachment from the end result of things. You may have found that you have questions that don't have answers, or perhaps you feel completely helpless because there was nothing you can do and there is still nothing you can do. Maybe the end result or verdict is out of your hands, yet you carry all of the emotions, weight, burden, stress, and possibly regret with no foreseeable "cure". This is most certainly an unhealthy place to be and one I wouldn't wish on anyone. When working with my clients I use a quote from *Deepak Chopra, The Seven Spiritual Laws of Success*

"In detachment lies the wisdom of uncertainty...in the wisdom of uncertainty lies the freedom from our past, from the known, which is the prison of past conditioning. And in our willingness to step into the unknown, the field of all possibilities, we surrender ourselves to the creative mind that orchestrates the dance of the universe.

While you may wonder how this is relevant, allow me to explain my understanding. Addressing the opposing view first, to live in certainty is to live trying to control the outcome and over time the need for always knowing can eventually lead to anxiety, stress and discontent. So that would mean that in the "wisdom of uncertainty" means being open to a new way of doing things and allowing them to be just so, and not expecting an outcome. Allowing what is in

135

our highest and best good to unravel and trusting in the Universe and of course, Karma.

Understanding how to utilize and combine the effects of forgiveness and detachment are paramount. At the same time being able to incorporate them into our lives going forward, will allow the building of a strong foundation for your new reality.

| Guiding Principals | Raison d'être | Feel the Pain | You Still Have To Matter | Be Vulnerable | Detachment |
| | Staying Present | Lean Into What You Love | Listen To Your Gut | | Share To Heal |

Seven – Choose your Warrior

Choosing how you will heal – Your Inner Warrior

It is absolutely okay not being or feeling okay, and I am not rushing your process or your timeline. I would like you to step outside of yourself for just a moment and try to determine what you might want to strive for being and feeling, as you continue finding your way on this path.

Take a long deep breath...close your eyes and imagine what you want to be like as you start to feel better, when you're thinking about life again and when you are designing what your new reality is going to entail. If it doesn't come easy, I understand. Shock, anguish, numbness, anger...all of the initial stages of the grief wheel are not easy places to be or to see your way clear for any length of time. That is where the Core Values & Guiding Principles come into play. By focusing and incorporating them in virtually

137

every thought, feeling and action, you are beginning to be proactive in your grief process vs. reactive. It can be exhausting at first, but well worth the time and attention.

It is completely normal during this process to move forward and still not feel awesome. Awesome will come again but I won't lie, it may be a little while. So, let's find a positive word that's more obtainable at the present moment. This is one of the many reasons I believe Sydney focused so heavily on "love". It's something we can very instinctively go back to that feels good, if even just for a moment. Love can eventually be awesome but for where we are right now, love is comfort.

In the journal entry that follows is about one of our final days together, a truly blissful moment for me that expresses everything about who Sydney and I were together.

May 24, 2017 Day 151 - *After Aubrey moved out (but not far away, which made me very happy), it wasn't often that when Syd and I were home that we weren't in the same room together. We would usually end our days in one of our rooms just lying around talking or watching a movie. And if I was working at the table and she was ready for us to be together, she would be sure to yell for me that it was time for me to be finished and to come hang out with her (she was the boss!). When we moved to the Trappe house, we downsized so the rooms were smaller so when I was in one room, and she was in another, it wasn't really like being in separate rooms. I mean, I could sit at the dining table and put my arm in the kitchen, to give you an idea of space. But yet, Syd would always make sure we were close. I so loved that. One night, within the last week of her precious life, she was in the kitchen baking away (one of her favorite things to do!) and I was at the table working...literally only a few steps away from her and she stopped what she was doing and made a declaration!!*

"Momma, why are you so far away?" Now, remember when I said I could sit at that table and extend my hand into the kitchen!! So I picked up my chair, along with my computer, and went and plopped myself directly in the middle of the kitchen!! I put my chair directly in front of the sink, (right in the way of "her" oven!) propped my feet up on the kitchen counter by the sink and sat back down and got back to work, I wanted to see what she would do to me! Squirt me, tickle me to get me out of her way, something! But instead, she turned to me and stopped what she was doing, paused and said, "now...that is much better!" with a big smile on her face. I can hear her voice and her laugh so clearly. Without hesitation, she got back to work happy to walk around me to get back to the oven to rescue her creation from the oven. She always just wanted to be with me and it didn't matter if it meant just laying on the floor with me and coloring as I typed out my notes from the day or if we played cards or worked on a puzzle as she told me about her day *or about a conversation she had with a friend or she would play music on her phone and see if I knew what the songs were. It was so amazing to me how easy it was for us to just be together and have it all flow so beautifully. When Aubrey and Kevin would come to visit, they very easily fell back into the ease of how things flowed when we were all together. It was really a terrific life.*

Now I take all of those incredible memories that I have been blessed with and cherish them but I am very careful to continue living in my present moment.

So, in keeping in the emotion of love, allow it to engulf you...take a deep breath, feeling all the love you have for your sweet child, for yourself and for the other people in your life that are depending on you. Take all of that overwhelming love and use that energy as fuel to see if you can see what "finished" can look like for you? How would you like to see yourself in a year? Then in

2 years and then maybe 5 years? Do you want to continue to be an example for your family? Do you want to feel whole again and find joy? Yes, I would say you would want all of that and more!

Stay in that moment as you read the next section and really dig deep into this feeling of love that surrounds you as you find your answers. It is critically imperative that you are HONEST WITH YOURSELF! There is no more rationalization and there is no more sacrificing. How do you want to move through this next year of your life?

I created 3 categories called "The 3 Warriors" and there is a dual role here with this next segment. It's meant as a bit of a warning of what could take place if you don't stay present and "in love" and also a great motivator of what is possible. I think you will see what I mean. When you read the definitions of all three, pay attention to how you are feeling as you read them. Does your stomach sink when you read one vs. flutter when you read another? Or maybe the hairs on your arms stand up? If that's the case, that's your gut telling you that is the warrior for you right now. This can always be revisited as you feel stronger, remember nothing is permanent. You have the option to change your mind at any time. Change for the positive. Whichever warrior you choose, you are setting an intention, which will be directing your thoughts and taking the appropriate actions necessary to bring that intention to fruition.

3 Warriors

Crusader Warrior - stays sad but has a smile, trying to say otherwise, but is vengeful becoming bitter, not better. Does advocacy work while staying in their pain vs. moving through it and finding peace. The advocacy work is how they appear to be making progress to the outside world but in reality, they are reliving their pain and allowing it to become their identity. They stay in pain, don't find complete peace and instead of helping others rise above their own pain, keep them down with them to suffer silently together.

Surviving Warrior – Survival mode is how these warriors choose to spend their remaining days, surviving but not able to move completely through the pain. They are not able to acknowledge the loss or any guilt or regrets they may have, which would allow them to heal and fall away. These warriors tend to stay sad with good moments, but do no advocacy. They stay in a place of lackluster and don't regain their spark.

Thriving Warrior - Starts in survival mode but realizes there is more in life and learns that it is ok to want more, and goes and gets it. Lives by example and finds how they can reach people to make a difference in the world with the gifts given to them. Accepting and embracing that life can be wonderful, even after the tragic loss of a child.

Intention

I learned early in my years of being a momma bear, the incredible influence I have on my girls and how much they depend on me and look to me. When my oldest daughter was the tender age of 3, she fell and needed 12 stitches in the back of her head. I remember her looking squarely in my eyes to see if there was fear or if there was calm in my eyes, at that moment I learned my role in life. It was to live by example, show them the way and help them find the courage they needed to take the next breath, listen to their gut, handle the hard situations with the balance of emotion and logic and keep a steady but forward motion.

So for me, and because of the way I am hard wired and all that I have already survived in my lifetime, I knew immediately that I wanted more than survival. I lived in survival mode for a brief time in my adult life and did not find it a rewarding place and it wasn't a place I wanted my girls to see as acceptable. I knew immediately that I wanted more, so I set the intention, using my raison d'etre as fuel when necessary. I was going to learn to thrive even though at that moment I could barely breathe.

This does not mean that you need to choose to thrive as your intention. You need to listen to what you need at this moment. If that means choosing survival as your goal, that is a very admirable place to start and I commend you for being so brave and trusting the possibilities, knowing how you are feeling at the present moment. Once you make this choice, write it down. Include it at the top of the list you have been creating from Chapter 6. Then write your raison d'etre alongside, so when you have a moment where you think you just can't go on, it is the reminder of why you are still here. This very easily brings you back to center, and with each reminder, hope slowly begins to form.

- ♥ Stay present throughout the process.
- ♥ Continue to incorporate the Basic Fundamentals.
- ♥ Focusing on the Core Values and Guiding Principles.
- ♥ Keeping your intention and raison d'etre top of mind.

These steps will help you move away from becoming a Crusader Warrior and help you continue to move forward in healthy ways.

Divine Time

Remember, it is completely okay with not being okay. Everything I have shared and will continue to share is not saying you don't have the right to not be okay. You definitely need to honor that, because it is a huge part of this process. What I am sharing with you is so that, in your time, which I like to refer to as divine timing, when you are ready to start feeling better, you will have a sense of direction. You will have had time to reflect on what you think you could want on the other side of the grief tunnel. The timing of when you feel that trigger of okay, I want to start feeling better, will happen differently than it did for me. I have a sense about you, that your hardwiring isn't too dissimilar to my own. You want your life back and as much as you want your baby back, you are realistic however and understand that is just not an option. In knowing that, you want to figure out how you can retain any kind of relationship with that beautiful soul that has gone, who now protects you from the heavens, and be okay with being okay with life again. Then, once you have a handle on being okay, I have this sense that you, too, are going to want to thrive! I am so proud of you for being okay with owning all of those feelings. You are a warrior and in time a thriving warrior!

Now to continue to fulfill your desire to become this thriving warrior, let's get back to some of the other ingredients necessary to support that. Earlier I mentioned setting your intention and end game or goal. Divine time is about going through this process, moving towards the intention that you have set, as it feels right to you. We all have our own divine timing within us and it is important that we honor it. Part of staying present ties to this as well, because it would be easy to quit or go slower than our usual way of doing things. Initially that is completely cool and acceptable. However, knowing yourself and getting back to your divine timing, will aid in a more natural process that best suits you. Hard to believe there could be anything natural about this process, I know. As you go through and incorporate what I have been sharing and keeping the speed in which you normally move in check, you will begin to see what I mean.

Release

Releasing is the next thing that comes to mind after discussing time. Partly because you will release things in your divine timing, but I have come to understand there is a particular way that releasing happens. With grief, in each and every step of the grief wheel, there is another process. This piece is where I have come to find most people, if not guided, can miss steps, and with that, find themselves later in life still harboring or holding onto something sad, negative and over time harmful to all the bodies; physical, mental, emotional, energetic and spiritual. I don't mean to scare you but I have seen what not being honest with yourself and not feeling the pain can do to a person over time. It is very sad and much harder to repair. This "other process" is like a set of stairs.

Let's start with the "firsts" you are experiencing. With each first you have to navigate how to survive, am I right? With each first, you experience multiple stages of the grief process all at once. So at any given time, you could be experiencing anguish, anger, a sort of numbness, disbelief and then, maybe there is even a shred of hope somewhere in there, if even only for a split second. Does this sound all too familiar to what you have been experiencing? It is how I remember my first year and all the "firsts" I had to go through.

These steps, I came to realize as I was working my way through each and every single "first", were a necessity. After the first year had passed, what I didn't bank on was that the "firsts" are not just the holidays and birthdays. They were also the little things that occurred each and every day that were painful reminders. Reminders that your sweet child is really gone and you are left here to put all the puzzle pieces back together, but strangely enough you have pieces from more than one puzzle. There are pieces to the puzzle still lingering from when your life was perfect and full and there are pieces to a new puzzle that is still left undetermined to what it will be. Your job is to identify and separate the puzzles and take note on the list you have been keeping for when you are ready to start designing your new reality.

Now, some of the pieces to the original puzzles just may fit in this new puzzle but you need to be very sure and pay very close attention to whether they line up and feel right. Otherwise, this new reality we have slowly been preparing ourselves for will be askew. The next chapter will provide you with the steps necessary to thoughtfully and proactively, in your time, gracefully move through each twist and turn vs. continue to react and find yourself stuck.

Karma

Journal entry – for the initial scheduling of the trial in December 2017 - *I have been reminded that on the day of Sydney's funeral I asked everyone to show this man kindness and I meant it then and I mean it now. I have been through every emotion as it relates to the defendant since the funeral and I can say I have come around full circle. It's one of the reasons I came up with "LOVE, forgiveness & Karma"* months back. I believe in choice & consequence and with consequence comes karma.

The "team" that is representing Sydney's best interest have been remarkable; compassionate people that are experts in their field. I like to say that Sydney chose them wisely! They are doing their best to prepare me and protect me from the ugliness that will unfortunately unfold and again, this takes me back to karma.

Karma will be served, whether in this lifetime or the next, and that is completely up to the defendant and the path he chooses to travel. Nothing that happens in that courtroom is going to bring Sydney back to us. And with that said, hosting bitter and vile thoughts or emotions towards the defendant will not harm him but it will harm you over time so please, find forgiveness. Forgiveness is something Sydney would want for you, for me. She would want us to carry her love and memory in our hearts and live life as she would; putting family *and friends before all else & living each day fully as if it were our last. Never put off what you can do today and embrace all that unfolds before you IN THE MOMENT.*

I will ask for each of you to hold hope in your hearts that the defendant will be brought to whatever the Universe deems in the highest and best good. For those of us that lost such a precious, pure soul, I hope that the Universe will provide us with some closure and help us find peace as we continue to figure out how to move forward and trust in karma.

The definition of karma is: bringing upon oneself inevitable results, good or bad, either in this life or in a reincarnation. There is something about this concept that provides me tremendous peace of mind. Perhaps it's a more politically correct way to say that someone will get what's coming to them, but I would like to believe it's a more evolved way to perceive cause and effect. It is an excellent gauge when making choices, for me anyway, because I believe in reincarnation and I truly do want to be the best person I am capable of being in all lifetimes.

Some people don't concern themselves with considering the consequences of their actions and this is where I find great comfort in the concept of karma. The reason I choose to add karma with the warriors and intention is because I believe that it is a conscious awareness in allowing karma to do its work. This enables me the ability to "detach" from the outcome of the trial and provides me the space then to continue to heal myself through "love", "compassion", "patience" and "forgiveness". Notice I did not yet include "honesty" with karma. The reason for that is simple. You can say you believe in karma but you need to be completely honest with yourself. It can't be just words. You need to FEEL your belief in karma. How, you ask? For me, it was when I came to understand that by my believing in karma, made me feel lighter somehow, like the weight of the world was lifted.

It allowed me to not hate, which is something that only hurts me in the long run. It seemed like the final step I was looking for in being able to live a life by example or "walking my talk".

It was the final step for me being able to be a thriving warrior. To thrive for me means to flourish, prosper, be successful and be happy. These are all things I would like to be or achieve in my lifetime. Knowing that about myself, I looked back over what was wrong or troubling in my life and decided it was time to let them all go. In doing so, I followed the process you have been reading to develop my plan to accomplish my goals.

That was a lot of information!! Whew!

Let's do a little recap;

♥   Be mindful and attentive in incorporating the Basic Fundamentals, the Core Values and Guiding Principles and you will begin to feel the direction this is taking you.

♥ Choose your warrior and choose how you want to travel through this journey.

♥ Set your intention.

♥ Understand this journey will happen in your time.

♥ Know that releasing is a very important piece to feeling whole again and also paves the way to invite the concept of karma into this process for you.

Choose Your Path | Intention | In Your Time | Release | Karma | Crusader Warrior | Surviving Warrior | Thriving Warrior

Eight - The 6 A's

6 A's; Acknowledgement, Allowing, Absorption, Acceptance, Adjustment & Adapting.

Journal entry - Day 337 – My birthday

Today is my birthday, something my girls always made special. In fact, my birthday, Mother's Day and believe it or not, Father's Day were 3 days that they took upon themselves to go out of their way for me, make me feel even more special then they already did on a daily basis. And even at a young age, they teamed up and conspired for me, finding their way through making us all dinner and then a beautiful birthday cake. It was beautiful to watch as well as receive. As they got older, they would tell me I wasn't allowed back in the house until a certain time so they could accomplish whatever they were up to and each year the meals and the cake became more elaborate (and more tasty ☺). Most years they made my card too. As a momma, it just doesn't get any better than that, quality time and knowing you are completely loved and appreciated.

This morning, as I was mindfully moving through a process I call the "6-A's" that I knew I was going to have to go through today (this is to show myself that I am, in fact, making progress. I never want to remain stuck!), I decided to honor Sydney by wearing one of her last gifts to me. Last Christmas, she and I went out shopping for the gifts she wanted to purchase for people. She was always very thoughtful about this and had specific things in mind for everyone. We had to do some searching but it was a successful and fun adventure. Then, when December 24th came and she was killed, everything stopped. I packed a bag and left our house and only went back again to pack to move. When we finally got to the point that we could unwrap the gifts that were under the tree to determine what to do with them, I found a box wrapped with my name on it. I took a deep breath and unwrapped it. In this box was the last few things she touched and found special for me. Everything in the box was so perfectly "me" and Sydney knew it. She was such a love. So, I took the shirt that says "Sunday is for Snuggling" , which is also my favorite color! (I tried wearing it once before but it was just too soon) and am wearing it today. It may sound silly, I mean it's only a shirt, but it's the principal and the significance behind what it stands for between her and I.

So this year, being a year of firsts, doing things without Sydney by our side or conspiring for us, has had its ups and downs. Today is my first birthday without her. Today is the first "momma bear's birthday" Aubrey is left without her sister, or partner in crime, to conspire. But I know we will survive! We are finding new ways together, sharing her love, memories and energy, to move forward on days like today but I think I speak for both of us when I say there is a hole or numbness. Perhaps that is grief's way to protect us as we go through the steps of the 6-

A's. What I have come to realize is that for EVERY first, you go through the 6 A's. It's not just a once and done process. So I think that for today's first, we have absorbed the reality, are adjusting and moving through the day by feeling gratitude and love. Before we close our eyes at the days end, we will have reflected on how blessed we all are by Sydney having been in our lives and now to have her watching over us.... and with that, "acceptance" will once again have taken us.

If you have done any searches on line you may have seen the 4 stages of grief; Acknowledgement, Absorption, Adjustment & Acceptance. Going through this process and speaking with clients that have also experienced this dreadful journey, I would say that yes, the A's are in fact real and you do go through them but I made two significant additions. First, there are two very important "A's" missing from the order, "Allow" and "Adapt". Acknowledgement is most definitely the first of the A's to introduce itself but following that is "Allow". You cannot "Absorb" what you have not "Allowed" to stir within you, let alone the loss of your child. Then, after you have had time to sit in "Allow" you can move to absorb and so on. So you and I are going to work with *6 A's; Acknowledgement, Allowing, Absorption, Acceptance, Adjustment & Adapting.*

The second difference I noted during the first year of my journey is that every single "first" I realized I was going to encounter, I needed to experience and move through the 6 A's each time. For example, the "first" book you find in a box that was theirs, a show on tv, someone dies in a movie, you hear a song, see one of their friends, drive by their favorite store or restaurant, etc. The list is endless.

Eventually it becomes easier but initially we fight each step. Breaking them down, one by one, may help with understanding some of the emotions that travel up the stairs of the 6 A's.

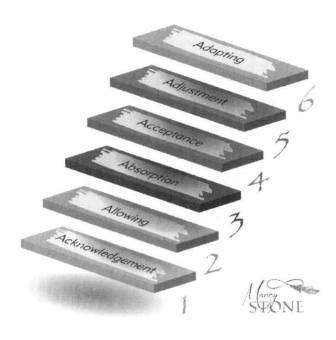

Acknowledge – somewhere in between the first two steps of the grief wheel; shock, anguish, denial and then numb, acknowledgement does in fact occur. That's part of why denial is in the first step. While we don't want to believe that our baby is gone, all of the facts say otherwise. We sometimes tend to fight the acknowledge step of the process.

Allow – this is "sitting in" what you now logically know you need to acknowledge. Feeling everything that flows through, staying present, and letting all of the flashbacks occur and the tears to flow.

Absorb – to retain, it is here that I found denial turns to disbelief, not to say that I didn't flux between them, but I knew being honest with myself and addressing "now what?" was paramount. I also often found that I would need to come back to this step almost like going up a step and then back down again, pause for a bit and then find the energy to go back up to the next step.

Accept – I would say this was, and is, absolutely the hardest step to take in the 6 A's process. To accept is providing consent, believing and recognize as fact. I felt like if I accepted that she was gone I was dishonoring her, but what I was really doing by not accepting was dishonoring her memory and not finding how to live the way she would want me to live. Each time I had to move through this step, I would have a chat with Sydney telling her that I am doing this for her and she was to let me know if I was moving in the wrong direction. So far, she has held up her end of that deal.

Adjust – another not so fun step. To adjust is to alter or move in a different way. This felt to me, initially, like I was giving up on Sydney, as silly as that sounds. If I started to adjust too quickly, will she feel, will others feel, like I am okay with all that is happening and just moving on? Those are real and just thoughts, but ones you need to move through and fast. They are counter-productive and the last thing you need is more to worry about. You have your hands full. I found myself taking the steps of this process always feeling that Sydney would want me to take the next step, and that helped me move forward. It also helps that I know Aubrey is watching and counting on me for the "how to" through this journey.

Adapt – to reconcile the new steps as they occur, and seeing how to incorporate them into the new every day. Sometimes I felt like I was stalling and not "owning" this and everything that is really happening. To finally make the adapting piece become real, meant I was adapting to Sydney being gone. That's a lot to wrap your head around. I brought in the love, took baby steps, initially, but eventually found my way.

The 6 A's is not a once and done process. I learned to do it in my own divine timing, not how someone or society told me they thought I needed to do it. Listening to my gut and staying present allowed me to find my way through these 6 A's as gracefully as I possibly could and still does to this day.

A journal entry from May 8, 2017 - *This weekend, going through a box from the move I came across the cards the girls have given me over the years (sentimental, yes I am) and the* top one was my Mother's Day card from last year. The girls always used one card and both wrote inside. And at every age, they always wrote such beautiful and heartfelt messages that will forever warm me. I realized again, at that moment that will be the final card from both of them. And it broke me again. A "first" and a "final", both in one breathe. I will admit, this one was very hard to find my way through. The pain you feel in your chest from the breaking, it really does feel like that, as if something inside you is splitting in two and you are helpless to stop it. But as I allow it to do what seems necessary, as crazy as that may sound, I know that on the other side of the breaking will be an eventual healing and understanding that I will survive. I have to believe that. And I want to be strong and show the people in my life that count on me that we will all be okay. Their love is felt through their pain of the loss they, too, feel and the void they look to fill.

Sydney was always all about family and was very clear about this throughout her life, at every age. She was so wise and understood that we are each others healing and in time, as we celebrate Sydney's life with more smiles and fun stories and less tears, her life's purpose of family & love will be our saving grace.

My first birthday and Mother's Day are perfect examples of my needing to go through the 6 A's and really process how I was going to make it through these days. All kinds of mixed emotions surfaced and I also had to remind myself of my daughter that will be with me celebrating these occasions. On both occasions, she was not sure how to behave and I could see that as soon as she came through the door. I hugged her and asked her if she was okay if we lit a candle in her sister's honor at dinner, so we could all be together. She was relieved that I had a plan, that I seemed to be doing okay and then through dinner I showed some emotion and shared stories so she and everyone else would know that it's necessary to emote. Now, as an event comes up, we decide how we want to move forward together and are starting new traditions because the old ones no longer feel good.

There are some days where I could have cried all day but then I take a deep breath and realize that really isn't going to do anyone any good and then I turn my emotion into something worthwhile and positive. Honestly, I often get this visual of Syd in heaven throwing jellybeans at me, or something, when I would over emote with tears and imagine her saying, *"come on momma, get a grip!"* Believe it or not, that helps me get out of my funk. She always had silly ways about her that were endearing and always brought me joy.

The toughest time of day for me is bedtime. Syd used to bring all of her pillows and blankets and snuggle up next to me every night until she turned 14. Then at 14, she would still come in and snuggle with me until I fell asleep and then she would go get in her bed. Our routine of her tucking me in every night lasted up until she was killed. She was 21. Bedtime is taking me the longest to figure out how to deal with and I still have my moments and I imagine it will never be considered easy.

I will tell you this, every ounce of my being is incredibly grateful to have those moments and if that means I have this pain, I will take the pain. Our love was overwhelmingly beautiful and it is how I am surviving, one memory at a time. I share that because in the first year of her being gone, I had to go through the 6 A's every single night. That lasted for quite a while and now at 16 months without her, I still have many nights where I am unable to look at her beautiful picture that's on my nightstand. Other nights I find myself feeling blue and I start sharing stories about her and her silliness, to help ease the pain of her not being draped over the foot of my bed talking me to sleep.

The first year, being a year of firsts, doing things differently, maybe numb or feeling less than whole has its ups and downs. Allow the emotions in but do not allow them to control you or overtake you. You will survive! You will find new ways together, sharing love, memories and energy at just the right time, to move forward on those "first days". The hole or numbness seems to come with trauma and perhaps that is grief's way to protect us as we go through the steps of acknowledgement, allowing, absorption, acceptance, adjustment and then adapting (6-A's). Through this year of firsts, be mindful of how you are feeling; do you want to give back, do you want to move, donate your material possessions, whatever comes to you be sure to weigh it carefully. Be extremely honest with yourself, especially during this time. If you are making the change to run and hide from whatever your trauma is, that is definitely the wrong thing to do and you will have regrets later. If you are making the change because it is what needs to happen next and now, then move mindfully through the change paying very close attention to what you're feeling, thinking and processing.

Understand that at this time of your life, EVERYTHING is different and you need to find a way to embrace it going forward. What you once knew about yourself is now different. You must reacquaint yourself with your new self and find your new center or balance in life. This is no easy task and it will take time. It requires patience, slowing down and the ability to be completely honest with yourself.

With each stair you climb moving through the 6 A's, there is a release or understanding that needs to occur in order to continue to move forward in healthy and embracing ways. How you intend, release and handle your divine time through each of the 6 A's and your mindset will be supported by which of the 3 Warriors you have chosen to be. All these things together will aid in who you will become for the next leg of your journey.

The 6 A's — Acknowledgement — Allowing — Absorption — Acceptance — Adjustment — Adapting

Nine – Communication & Paving the Way

Let's do a quick recap on the "take a ways" covered so far that are guidelines to help you navigate;

♥ **Basic Fundamentals** – things to help you regain your balance and remain healthy as you travel through this tunnel of darkness, into the light.

♥ **Core Values** - what we expect from others and ourselves. They shape your world in altruistic and benevolent ways. Core Values provide direction on how to treat one another.

♥ **Guiding Principles** – concepts, thoughts and actions when daily & mindfully incorporated, along with the lifestyle suggestions, will provide proactive direction into what comes next for you, now and moving forward.

♥ **Your List** – this consolidates your observations of what no longer works for you in your life; relationships, material possessions, jobs, your personal style, even where you live.

♥ **Choosing your Warrior** – how you will move forward and how to ease the process of releasing and in your own time.

♥ **Intention and goal** – declaring these to proactively prepare for when you begin to see the light at the end of the tunnel.

♥ **The concept of karma.**

♥ **The 6 A's.**

All of the things listed above will help you navigate through this incredibly unfortunate turn of fate and they are also helping shape your new reality.

Another journal entry from May 8, 2017

I used to believe that losing a child would be the hardest thing in life to endure. Now I have come to realize that while the loss is unbearable, it's the survival after the loss that completely breaks you, totally pushes you over the edge. Because now you are not only dealing with the incredible void or hole that is left within you from losing this special bonded love, but, now...how you viewed life; what mattered, how you think, speak, act, dress, and view the big picture of life...all of those things, and then some, are no longer as you knew them. You are now a completely different person and not only do the people around you not know you but you yourself are searching to understand who you are now, and becoming, from this incredible tragedy.

Simplicity has been key for me. I have let go of virtually everything material that was me, then. Some things I can't even imagine using, doing, wearing or even going to anymore. The things I kept are things that we, Sydney, Aubrey and I had a connection to. Certain pieces of clothing or blankets that were cherished remain so.

Pictures, although most I am unable to look at yet, are the biggest piece of what I have clung to. Memories, these are joyful yet painful but I allow myself to flow there to ensure I don't let the pain of now outweigh the joy we experienced together then.

Everyday there is a new "first" of what this new reality of mine, ours, looks like. Everyday I willingly shed a tear (or two) to not only honor the memory but to also ensure I am allowing the pain to flow freely so it doesn't hold me prisoner forever. With each tear, I somehow find a way to move through it, knowing not only that I am going to survive, but that I remain here on this earth with a purpose. The purpose piece is truly what keeps me strong. It is one of my tether's to sanity for the here and now. And one Sydney and I shared...

As we start to focus on your new reality, the phrase or concept, "when everything changes, change everything" comes to mind. Below is another journal entry that I will share with you because it may help you. I needed to allow this honesty within myself in order to begin to truly find my way with my list and moving forward.

There is a concept, "when everything changes, change everything", and it speaks volumes to me. When I initially heard this, it made sense to me having gone through a divorce and becoming a single mom, no momma bear and feeling the truth of the words through each day. But I can tell you now, looking back over this last 16 months of my life, having lost Sydney, its only now that I really TRULY get the full meaning of the statement. After my divorce, many things changed around me but the depth of what has changed within me now vs. then is profound. When I looked in the mirror after the divorce, I saw the woman that wanted things like (but not limited to); to continue to be a strong role model for her young girls, teach them the beauty of independence and strength, be successful in business and show the girls that we could accomplish anything we intended. That person has always been at the depth of my core and while these traits are still very strong within me, how I get there has changed completely. First, I realized that those things I mentioned above are not things I strive to be because they are intrinsic to my core being, meaning I was hard wired this way. I did not need to work hard, that came natural for me. It was only to the degree in which I felt I needed to carry these traits out or to strive to take them to a different level that any effort may have been needed. So while these core traits are still within me, things that seemed important to me then have drastically altered. The very fabric or texture of my core is different.

How I see things is very different and what I am willing to let go of has increased considerably. The value of things, and sadly, even some people is drastically different. I never was big on material possessions, to the point if someone said they liked a painting, lamp, chair, necklace, etc. that I had, I gave it to them, but now I could live out of a backpack in my car. I used to believe that I stood in my power but today I see my level of inner power has been enhanced to a place that is taken me quite a time to adjust to in order to get comfortable in this new skin. I say what I mean so much more clearly than I have in the past and in the past I thought I was doing a good job. I stand up for myself in ways I thought I was before, only now it feels like there isn't another option, it just is. I no longer rationalize with myself, I just know it is or is not going to be. I also hear people differently. I hear what they aren't saying as they speak.

But this "everything changes, change everything" thing goes so much deeper than I could ever have imagined. Some are simple things yet, if I wasn't paying attention, I might have missed. Things like the foods I like or used to like. The music I like now vs. what I used to enjoy. This has changed to the point that some of the music I used to like overwhelms me.

Activities that used to catch my attention for hours now no longer interest me. Fashion, I used to love to have options of the eras because I felt I could pull off many styles and now I have cut down to the basics. I am still interested in fashion but when it comes right down to it, I realize in the grand scheme of things, it is inconsequential. These are the things we allow ourselves to get caught up in as humans, to deflect the need to go deeper, to keep us from feeling what really matters, to block our depth perception like a boat in murky water. You can only see so far and unless you have the courage to move farther than you can actually see or feel, you never get to that next level of "real" but instead stay in the safe zone.

Some of the things that I have been realizing lately are things that I never in a million years would have thought to be things that would be affected during this "change everything" process. Physical touch: this is something I never would have imagined would change but *for the longest time I did not want to be hugged or touched. I just needed to be in my own space. Then being kissed was something that took a while to be okay with again, oddly enough. The intimacy, I suppose is what is in question. Am I worthy of being loved and intimate when my baby will never have that chance again? Am I willing to be that open again with someone? Am I even ready to be open enough with myself, let alone be that with another being? Then I came to realize once I surpassed that milestone that then all of my intimacy triggers are no longer what they once were. Even after having the chat with myself and being ready to be intimate again, I still came to realize that many things that once worked for me intimately no longer do, and I am now in the "changing everything" exploratory phase of my love life. Some could look at this and be distraught thinking there was something wrong with them, but it made me realize the truth behind the depth of how far you change and learn how to honor this new version of yourself. For a short while, I thought*

I was broken, that my "muchness" was gone but then my husband told me that I needed to be kind to myself and allow what was happening to happen and not judge it or me. Something I would have most definitely have said to my clients. We all need to hear these words at some point in our lives and we need to be open to receiving them. This also took me awhile to be ready to do. I was fine receiving the guidance, but receiving kindness from myself was definitely hard to do at first, but as I did then things started to happen in a more graceful manner.

All the changes mentioned in my journal entry above are definitely not easy steps to move through, and take time, but there is something that happens to us as people when we lose a child. At first it feels like an all-encompassing numbness that overtakes us in the very first months of our loss, which in time turns to an ongoing disbelief. Then there is a slow subtle shift in what now matters to us and that is not just the grief talking. It is the depth of our humanity that we are able to feel once the grief has stripped us of all things we thought used to matter and now find to be trivial. Things that surface that have been buried or blurred are now finding their way again to the surface as we stay present and allow the pain to flood us. In feeling the pain, the love that we feel is so much deeper than we could ever imagine.

Grief makes you understand the power of love. Grief gives you the opportunity to become better than you ever were and provides you with a reason to do just that. Grief can become your platform for becoming that incredibly unique person you were meant to be. Grief no longer allows you to blend in. <u>Please do not take this as me being grateful for my grief, I am not.</u> I do, however, understand that this is where my life's journey has brought me. I can choose to be the crusader warrior and suffer silently or I can make the call to grief and say I will take on your challenge and I will show grief no mercy.

As you come to identify with all of what is occurring within you that stems from your loss, you are able to start to feel your way through what truly matters now, good, bad or indifferent. When you start to feel your way through the things in your journal entries and how you would like them to be going forward, you are contributing to your new reality. Using the steps in the 6 A's will make each decision a little easier, but it is not a fast or overnight process. Things like intimacy, involvement, attention, patience, honesty and allowing yourself to be okay with getting back into life, all these will all take time. Be patient with yourself and be vulnerable enough to communicate what you are feeling with the people that need to know. This will help keep your relationships moving forward together.

Communication

If you notice, communication has not been listed as any of the elements and there is a reason for this. Communication is incredibly important and is WITHIN every single element of this process. Every bubble would have communication listed within it. When you are expressing love and being honest with yourself, you are communicating. When you are leaning into love, you are communicating and the same goes for every single "bubble" on the Grief Process Overview in the following chapter. I created this chart for you to see an overview of everything you just read and will hopefully be easy to digest in one picture to see how it flows.

Communication, being honest and going with your gut are going to be instrumental in how you move forward with your list: your new reality. Again, I go back to relationships. There are going to be relationships, even family, that are not going to understand what you are doing, why you are doing it or even how you are doing it. That's okay, it's inevitable. Change is hard for people and by you making changes in your life means they are being asked, subliminally, to change as it relates to their relationship with you. They either can or they don't have to. It is their choice and you will need to honor whatever they decide.

I recall having my communication feel so crystal clear to me that it made it hard for some people to comprehend. As I look back, my delivery was probably incredibly blunt and could have been misunderstood. Again, there were so many things that seemed to matter before that no longer are of any concern. In the heat of the first year of raw and tattered emotions, it was hard sometimes to listen to what some people thought as pertinent, that I now saw as irrelevant. Unfortunately, because I felt like I was reacting to things like perception and judgment, there were times that I probably responded in incredibly angry ways throughout the first year. I was not considering delivery as much as I was trying to keep it all together and listen to what was screaming out to me about what was going to be my new reality.

In hindsight, I did not spend time considering the relationship between communication, compassion, perception and judgment. I now understand that **when communicating, there is always a perception and in that second you are given a choice.** You can choose to demonstrate compassion, realizing that you have no idea what the other person is going through and giving them the benefit of the doubt. Or from perception you can choose judgment, which provides no compassion, which will forever alter the ability to communicate, let alone communicate unconditionally.

Now with some time having passed, I realize what I now see...is life, without the sheaf of rationalization that we sometimes create to make ourselves feel better about something that is happening in our lives.

This also made it easier for me to identify where to begin in executing the changes I needed on my

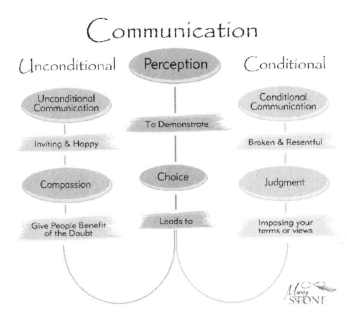

Communication

Unconditional	Perception	Conditional
Unconditional Communication		Conditional Communication
	To Demonstrate	
Inviting & Happy		Broken & Resentful
Compassion	Choice	Judgment
Give People Benefit of the Doubt	Leads to	Imposing your terms or views

list. Easier for me maybe, but not necessarily easy for the people around me. What I have to offer about that is, kindly communicate what you need to do for your new highest and best good but do not feel the need to explain yourself. This is your life. You don't see them explaining to you why they thought it was important to buy a bigger house or buy a new car. Do what you need to do for you.

Through this journey, being brutally honest with myself, removing all rationalizations and peacekeeping measures, I realize the people that have remained in my life are here because they love me to my core, along with all my flaws, quirks and silly habits. They don't care why I do something as long as they see that I am a happier version of me now that I made the change. They support my stages through this process and don't judge me. I have watched that list dwindle into the single digits over the last 16 months, but that is okay. I hold no ill will towards anyone that has needed to leave. I would rather them go then stay and hinder my new reality with negativity and judgment. This is very important to understand. This is your life and you are surviving, no, thriving, with the loss of your baby and they have absolutely no idea what is involved. I hope for their sake, they never do.

"Unconditional"

Unconditional means without limits. Like

communication, this is a concept that feel needs to be addressed and also added to every bubble on the Grief Overview Process. The world needs more unconditional acts of kindness, compassion, honesty, forgiveness, loyalty, patience and love...and you still matter, unconditionally. You unconditionally love your sweet child, and it is because of that love that motivates you to find your way. Do so with as many "unconditionals" as possible. Be unconditionally honest with yourself, communicate unconditionally, show no limits and feel no barriers.

By lifting these self-imposed obstacles, you are staying true to keeping your heart open and feeling everything. As time passes you will start to have many days where you will be able to feel past the pain. As you travel more into the "Service & Hope" stage of the grief process and begin acting on a few of the tributes you want to set into motion for your beloved baby, new emotions will surface. Allow them, do not suppress them. That serves no one, least of all you and definitely not what your sweet child would want for you. This is all a part of the new reality that is dawning within you. Invite the newness; thank your sweet baby for being with you through this journey and for the confidence in being okay with being okay with this new arrangement of sorts.

Walking this earth knowing you now have a direct link to heaven can be bittersweet. However, you will feel a sense of calm when you embrace it and are unconditional with it moving forward. I talk to Sydney all the time. Sometimes out loud and other times in my head. In fact, the other day I was on my way to lunch to meet an old friend, who is grieving the loss of her dear sweet mother, and I was running late (because I was writing!) and I was coming up on the exit I needed and a truck was puttering along so I just said, "if you could get this truck moving or out of the way, that would be super!" and within my next inhale, the truck put on his blinker and went into the other lane. I just smiled, chuckled, and said "thanks honey". Sydney always did like my friends! I tell you this because it is a part of living unconditionally. I, unconditionally trust that she is with me and will always be with me. Even those days where it feels she is quiet, she is always with me. So take the "unconditional" rule into every single aspect of your life. **Live unconditionally**. This will lead to living with no regrets.

Ten – Here's to life - Service, Hope & a New Reality

So here's to changing everything...

The first 9 chapters have covered the anguish, the loss and the steps around finding your way through, in hopes of someday feeling ok, then good, then maybe even great is possible. I can tell you that being at the 16-month mark of my loss, I have days with all of those, including some great days. Initially, I started out having bad days but I wouldn't allow them to last long and mindfully changed my verbiage to having good days with bad or sad moments. Now I am having some great days with sad moments and I embrace those sad moments. They keep me focused on my gratitude for life, for the love we had then and now, as she stays by my side nudging me forward with her signs and through dreams.

Now it feels time to discuss the final stages at

greater detail. You will see some things already covered earlier, and that stands to their level of importance and how everything in this process crosses over the other, and will always remain appropriate and important.

Service

I believe acts of service to be an important element in this journey. It allows you to get out of your own grief, even if just for a little while, to do something to help someone else that may be in trouble, have trauma or just need a friend. Otherwise we can get so caught up in our own sorrow and spin out of control or worse, fall down into the black hole of misery. Providing simple and kind acts of service can negate the deep dive into the black hole. If you are in need, here are a few ideas to get you started. You can offer your time with a local charity or soup kitchen. Check the obituary section of the newspaper, see if there is an elderly person that just lost their life long partner and reach out to them and maybe prepare and deliver a meal for them.

Perhaps there is a children's hospital nearby, go to the terminally ill floor with gifts for the children. Watch how you light them up and remind yourself as you do, that these children understand they are going to die and yet they smile.

These are just a few suggestions of how to serve and free yourself of your own trauma, even if only for an afternoon, and see how different you feel. It is also an excellent mental resource for days that you are feeling low. You can recall the smiles and gratitude on the faces of the people you blessed with kindness and love. We are all going through something in our lives, please never think that your pain is worse than someone else's. Please don't compare. Just understand that no matter what the pain, a kind gesture can do so much for all parties involved.

Service at this juncture is identifying whether or not you have it in you to start a movement, either now or in the future. I am not asking you to create the next Facebook or get out there and become a political activist. What I am suggesting is perhaps your sweet love was a budding genius or excellent at a particular sport or video game. There is always some way you can pay tribute to what moved them by donating your time or starting a foundation or even a scholarship in their honor. I have found this to be an amazingly healing form of giving back while honoring and keeping the memory of my sweet Sydney alive. As an example we started a culinary scholarship in Sydney's honor because that was her passion and it would give her great pleasure in knowing that every year there is a kid out there that might not have been able to fulfill their dreams if it wasn't for "her ability" to help. We have also started a "Yoga for Recovery" program for those individuals involved in their rehabilitation. They want to live a better life and I commend them for their courage to figure out how to do that and my

hope for them is that they find peace on their new path. I know for me, being a small part of their healing path brings me a level of peace I wasn't sure I would find again without her here with me.

We will continue to find and/or create ways to give back and find organizations or charities that would have resonated with what Sydney believed in. I also plan to find ways to help decrease the possibilities of momma bears experiencing what you and I are...our greatest nightmare.

Hope

Hope is something that feels desperately needed in this process because sometimes the leap to faith can be a challenge. Hope can take all forms; I hope that yoga helps in people's recovery, I hope that whoever acquires the culinary scholarship uses it wisely and becomes all they were meant to be, I hope that I will remain in forgiveness during the criminal trial, I hope to be able to make a lasting impression on you so that you will start to really live again and be okay doing so. Hope. In some ways I have graduated to faith; I have faith that Sydney is with me every day, I have faith that Aubrey is going to continue to heal and live a good and happy life, even with missing her sister and I have faith that you can feel good again. My faith in a higher power is why I am even still here, walking this journey. But in many places, I remain in hope and I am good with that. I have many years left and will work on turning my hopes to faith, in my divine timing. My hope for you now is that you will take action and start with love and identifying your raison d'etre, your reason for living. I have faith that if you do, the rest will flow a little easier for you as you travel this path with me.

Commemorative Tribute

The next step, while it may seem similar to that of service, it takes on a more personal feeling. Establishing a **Commemorative Tribute** to and for your sweet baby could be one or many acts. I have found this to be incredibly helpful, especially during the first year of loss. By bringing people together that loved her and hearing their stories provided a fullness and energy that I was able to carry and ride for a good long time after the event. Trust me when I say there were many days that I needed to tap into that loving energy to help me through moments and sometimes days.

Often sharing a memory on Facebook with my friends helped me feel ok in that moment. Sometimes people would provide comments that also helped and it kept us connected. We decided to spread Sydney's ashes when we traveled. She loved to travel and particularly loved when there was a beach involved. She was definitely a beach lover. In sprinkling her ashes where we knew she would enjoy being if she were here, made me feel good for some reason. It's as if I am helping her complete her quest of unfinished business on her bucket list. I hope she smiles down on me each time that we do.

I'm sure I have already mentioned her birthday, another monumental day for us. The first one without her, I honestly wasn't sure how I was going to get through the day. But we found a way. We hosted a "Celebration of her Life" event where she used to work. Many of her friends still work there and asked, *"where do we go to sit with her to pay our respects and talk to her"* because she does not have a plot. We decided to have an aqua blue Adirondack chair made, with a dedication plague, and left it "on the beach" where she worked. Her employer was fabulous about it and I still receive pictures of family and friends "visiting her" in her chair. I also have had pillows made from her t-shirts and I'm in the process of finding someone to create lap quilts with some of her other clothing...there are so many ways to keep our loved ones alive and close to us.

Partial journal entry from September 7, 2017 – Happy Birthday my love

Sydney would have been 22 years young today. She always loved her birthday. Not because of gifts but because of the changes it signified in the year to come. She looked forward to all that each year was going to allow her to explore, along with the endless possibilities and adventures. And let's not forget it meant MORE quality time together! And cake!!! She loved cake (and cheesy fries)!

It is so hard to imagine having been without Sydney's beautiful smile, infectious laugh, sarcastic wit and her deep love for me, her family and friends and all she believed in. It's still so hard for me to wrap my head around the fact that she isn't going to come running through the door with some crazy story and that laugh!

We decided to take a bit of Sydney to share her with the world in a place she would love, Delray Beach, Florida. We had a tough time deciding on the beach or the inter-coastal waters but when we found a small private beach and watched all of the boats go by, we knew we found her spot. You see, Sydney loved being out on the boat with her grandparents and cousins when she went to the beach. And this past summer, her Poppi was teaching her how to manage the boat and she was SUPER excited about this. LOVED IT!!!

So, at sunset and low tide, Ken and I took some of her ashes and put her in the water as a boat went by and she went out with its wake. She would have been thrilled!!! It was a very hard and emotional thing to do but it feels necessary on so many levels. She is so worth it and was so happy traveling and being by or on the water. She just sparkled more than ever during those moments. And if you knew her, you knew she ALWAYS sparkled.

I would like to personally thank our friends in Delray for allowing us this opportunity. I will forever be grateful and thankful. It was a moment we will never forget...

Happy Birthday my sweet girl. Love knows no limits, from here to there...wherever you may be flying off to today, this day of yours, September 7th.

I am 100% positive that you have those same feelings and love for your sweet baby, so share! Tell the world and as you relive the memories you will feel your heart swell with pride and love. I believe celebrating her life to be something I will do over the remainder of my days and, as you would guess, not just on her birthday. There is just so much of her to share and so many people that want to share her. So much so that it has become a stand-alone step and one that I hope you embrace. The feelings that are experienced with every act is fuel to enable you to keep moving forward and remembering and honoring the space between the dashes.

Defining your new reality

That short sentence is a fully loaded statement. One you have been subliminally moving towards throughout the chapters. The list (from Chapter 6) you have been creating and tracking is the groundwork for what your new foundation needs to look like going forward. Please remember, if you are feeling comfortable right now, you need to rethink your list. As crazy as this sounds, it's the discomfort that lets you know you're on the right track.

You have been keeping track of your observations of what no longer works for you in your life; relationships, material possessions, jobs, your personal style, even where you live. You will be incorporating all of what you have covered thus far in this step of the process. Take the 6 A's for example, they will be instrumental in how you identify what is next for you. Some examples of things that needed to change for me were mentioned in the prior chapter in my journal entry but to reiterate a few; food, music, fashion, intimacy and most of my relationships. All of these things have been dramatically affected and changed since that fateful day. For me, I found that making many of these changes as I was in the moment was necessary for me but this is because I was very in tune with myself prior to losing Sydney. If I was not so aware, I may have waited to make some of the changes but I made many of my changes throughout the first year. There were also many things that required time in order to make the change I needed in this next leg of my journey so I have laid out the necessary steps and an appropriate timeline to feel like I was making progress.

I know that I said to be extremely careful to make any wild or sudden changes within the first year. While I made a number of significant changes within my first year of losing Sydney, it reminds me that I am really only a few months into what I would consider actually feeling some comfort in what I have been redefining for myself, and it will continue to morph. With that, I have been trying to determine the best course of action in sharing what it can look like or even feel like, keeping in mind, your journey will definitely be different, but an example is sometimes helpful. Sharing seems to be something I am growing comfortable with, yet I will say to share the now vs. the first year of my loss, feels different somehow. Perhaps because I feel less of "an expert" in the new reality aspect of this journey, but I will do my best in providing a few examples and will do so from my "list".

I will take examples from there starting with what was the biggest and most critical for me at the time; moving and parting with material possessions. I did not go back to the townhouse where Sydney and I were living, except to gather clothes and even then I was put on a timer by my then fiancé so I wasn't there too long because it tore me apart being in "our" space. It was the reminder of the knock on the door and every fabulous memory would flood over me. It only took me about 5 minutes to become an absolute mess. I immediately started the process of how to "get out" and yes, in a sense I was running, but I knew my fiancé' had my best interest in mind and wasn't going to let me do anything silly or let anything happen to me. I have no regrets on never sleeping in that place again. I have never regretted moving. I KNEW I wasn't going to have regrets. It was so very clear to me that it was the only way for me. My gut told me loud and clear and everything else inside me that could "tell me" agreed. Getting out was the only way.

So, if you are considering moving from the home you created with your sweet baby and every ounce of your being is saying "do it!" then that is your answer. There can be no doubt. That is such an important inner gauge: **there can be no doubt**. It's not your will kicking in, or the need to run, it isn't anything other than simply and unequivocally KNOWING! If you have any hesitation, then wait. Make plans but continue to pay attention to your gut. If you are holding on to the old things or ways as a safety, sentimental reasons or fear, I completely understand. Just ask yourself, what would my angel say to me right now? Would they want you to linger in the past? Or would they want you to bring pieces of the past with you as you move forward and live with the love you have for them, and them for you? I just knew for me that staying in that house, alone, was the absolute worst thing I could have done. You will know.

Another example of what no longer served was material possessions. Like I said before, Sydney was not one for material things and that had to come from somewhere! When we were at the house packing the bare essentials, I would look around and it was like I was looking at someone else's furniture. None of it had any feeling or attachment, except in Sydney's room. No surprise there, I'm sure. So, with the exception of some of my clothes, all of Sydney's clothes, some of her more sentimental things from the kitchen (she was a foodie, remember) and her bedframe, everything else was donated. I just knew I would be fine without all of it and quite honestly, it is all replaceable, its just stuff.

I will admit two things, first it is pretty freeing not being beholden to material possessions, meaning I have my priorities straight and...there are one or two things that I might have wanted to keep, but the thought passed fast and I didn't replace it anyway. Its just stuff and now that I am thinking more clearly, it makes me feel good that somewhere out there someone is enjoying what they might not otherwise been able to afford.

As long as you listen to your gut, stay present and are honest with yourself, these changes will be much easier to make than they might have been before you lost your baby. I have come to realize that I see the value of things differently than I once did and initially I was not feeling okay about this. What I mean by that is that I have a different view of the world.

Being okay with closure in relationships

Once you lose a child, it can be difficult to relate to many people. The things they worry about or that seem to be of great importance, you now see as trivial. Its nothing against them, it's the difference between what you have survived and how that has changed you. Being okay with all of the things that are now different about you and within you is part of what you need to embrace. The changing of my relationships was one of the

211
The Voice of an Angel

most difficult things for me to navigate as I was rewiring and reworking my life to fit the new me. Many people around you will struggle with this and they may fall away, especially if you are dealing with your loss in ways that they can't comprehend. I had someone tell me I was headed for a nervous breakdown because I wasn't allowing myself to grieve. I read this to mean that this was their perception according to how they would imagine they would grieve. Comparing, being judged and people assuming things has been a very common and sad reality during this journey. My process is and will be different than anyone else's and is different than yours.

So by now you are aware of who decided to move on and allow yourself to be okay with what is happening. This is and was one of the hardest pieces of this journey for me. Many of the people that have been in my life the longest and I was sure they would be with me through everything are the ones that walked or fell away. Trying to make reason or rational sense of it is sometimes impossible. Sometimes they are square with you and say "I can't be the kind of friend you need me to be" and then they go. There is a level of respect that comes with that, at least they gave you that...closure. With everything else in your life right now that has so many raw and ripped nerve endings, closure in one place is good. So, don't fight this process and don't stay upset about it or with the individuals. Allow the energy to flow and keep moving forward.

Some people may go into their own grief, guilt or regret, which does not allow them to be there for you. As I go back through my handwritten notes, when I just started writing and was in the first raw months, I was angry and hurt. People were falling away and leaving me at the time of my life that I felt I needed them the most. I felt betrayed and hurt because I thought these people cared about me. I was there for them in their time of need and now that it's my turn, I look around and they are nowhere to be found. I felt them selfish and our relationship one sided. Now, months later, seeing and hearing things a little more level headed and not as emotional as before, I would say that perhaps those people were simply trying to honor where they were in their journey.

As hard as it may be at the time, you may come to realize that by these individuals being present for the grief and loss you are experiencing, may be triggering events or experiences that they may have had and not fully healed from or pushed down. You are making them uncomfortable or sad or even angry. Your "stuff" is making them feel and look at their "stuff".

So, honor them for standing in their place. This may mean they "see" what they may have missed and now are in a better place or time to start to deal with it. This is a gift in a way. It is helping someone else see what he or she couldn't see before in his or her own life. That is not something to take lightly. So, be kind to them if they need to walk away from you. Honor the place they are in and thank them for being honest with you.

Lingering Limitations

Don't let things that don't feel right or you can't bring yourself to do just yet become issues. This is perfectly normal and you need to honor where you are. These things will change over time but forcing them will only make it more painful and you have been through enough. I have a few things that I feel slow in overcoming, and I am not thrilled about it, but it's where I am in my journey, so I need to be kind to myself and honor my timing.

When I would be having conversations with people, I would always ask them about their children; how many do they have, their ages, what are their hobbies, etc. Watching people discuss their children is great because all of the sudden this really serious, stodgy business person is all business and then bamm! The expression on their face changes instantly and while a little guarded at first, they start to become almost animated and it's beautiful to watch. You can learn a lot about a person in how they share about their children. I always loved sharing about my girls, I am so proud of them and all that they are. Now, I find myself answering the return inquiry with, "I have two beautiful girls, 25 and 21" and leave it at that, hoping they won't ask for more details. It's not that I am ashamed, not at all. Telling people about my daughters ends in immediate silence now AND it feels as if my beautiful 25 year old becomes forgotten!! I never want to out shadow Aubrey and am very mindful that she continues to realize how incredibly special and smart she is. So, this right now is one that I am still working through in this new reality.

Another lingering limit is I will not travel on the road of the accident or through the town where it occurred. To utilize the road where she was killed, which was a shortcut of ours, seems insensitive and disrespectful. To travel through the town would mean I would have to pass the exact site of the accident and I just don't want to do that. It was that I couldn't, I was afraid I would see blood on the street or those fake flowers people put up at accident sights. The thought of her being remembered at an accident sight feels so limiting and so harsh. That could just be my momma bear protector kicking in. She was so much more than fake flowers at a street sight grave marking. I am still working through this and I am okay with it being a limiting factor right now. That would feel like I forgot or it was inconsequential or it didn't matter if I traveled on that road. Again, this is my stuff and where I am at 16 months into my journey and navigating this new reality. I share these things so when something surfaces for you that feels like you "should be" farther along, you don't do that to yourself. Everything happens in your time. You have come a long way.

Trying to embrace this new reality

As you go through your "List", you may have some things on there you didn't enjoy or do at all, prior to this devastating loss, but now all of a sudden, those things seem to be finding their way to you. Don't overlook them, try them. Yep, get out of your box and give it a go! There could be something that you need to experience within a particular event, hobby or outing, whether you realize it or not and that is why it is surfacing. Like belly dancing! Yes, belly dancing.

Some positive changes I have been making over the past few months are things I never did before and never thought I ever would and that means taking my first belly dancing class. For those that know me, you realize how huge this is! One of my dear friends has been teaching belly dancing for as long as I have known her and she was always asking me to try it out. No, no, no, it's just not my thing. What was my thing you say? Well, I was the one that everyone comes to if they needed something, the responsible one, just like Syd. But Sydney had a much better handle on her ability to be light. I used to call her my fun factor. Seriously. She would dance around the house and sing silly to the lyrics of a song to make me laugh. I could be silly with her but it was/is not my go to behavior. So belly dancing was in that fun factor category and my fun factor is gone. In this new reality of mine, with my fun factor now watching over me, I decided to throw caution to the wind and take my friends' class. She was overjoyed and knowing me as well as she does, did a fabulous job at getting me to relax and release and flow without me even realizing it was happening. I approached it like it was a project or process I needed to understand, because this was a safe path for me. Now before I go on, know this about me. I have no problems jumping into anything new and can be considered a bit of a risk taker. This, however, was different and it took me a while to figure it out.

To belly dance, I needed to throw my physical self out into the world and I have always had issues with expressing my physical being, like through dance. That's drawing a kind of attention to myself that makes me uncomfortable. I believe it goes back to the concept of being judged. People judge and that is something I have dealt with my entire life so I realize now, I stopped putting myself out there in that capacity. I created a boundary for myself in my prior life.

Back to belly dancing, now that I realized I had a self-imposed boundary, I knew what I needed to do. I did what made me COMPLETELY uncomfortable, I belly danced. Well, I attempted to anyway. And you know what, it was fun and a great ab workout! Will I belly dance again? Probably under my friend's supervision, and then who knows what will unfold, but I was proud of myself for pushing myself to be uncomfortable to be a better and more diverse me. I am 100% sure that Sydney was watching with a huge grin on her face joining in with some of her famous moves.

The next fun thing that I did was I "went Rogue". Rogue is a mutant/superhero in one of the XMen movies... we loved those movies. We, I, specifically loved Rogue's hair. At the end of the movie, she had a long gray streak that framed the one side of her face. She looked quite beautiful so I joked and said to Sydney that when I was in my 50's and have the gray hair coming in, I am going to go Rogue. She said she was going to hold me to that. Well, Sydney won't be here for my 50th birthday. So last fall, I jumped the gun completely and went Rogue. I needed a change and while this may sound a little silly, I wanted to see a reminder of her every day. I now have this atomic blond streak and I think it's quite fabulous. I am also allowing the rest of my hair to slowly gray, for now anyway. Remember, nothing needs to be permanent. Going gray is something I never would have done years ago. Never! But through this journey of loss, recentering and rebirth into a new reality, so much of what seemed important back then doesn't any longer. Who cares if I go gray? I believe anyone can pull off any look, it's all in your attitude and how you carry yourself that matters. Go big or go home! So many people have commented on the look and are now considering the concept of embracing who they are at every age vs. running from the number. It's a small part of living by example for me and honoring Sydney's and my plans.

Every day I think about where I am in my journey in this new reality. Some days I am pleased with my progress and other days I feel like I am not doing enough. This is normal and I am sure you will have days that you feel similarly. The key is to find patience for yourself. Sometimes you may need to remind yourself that your original reality was years in the making and was altered in the blink of an eye. This new reality will take some time to fit and may need a few alterations as you move forward. Continue to pay attention, stay present and keep the 6 A's handy. Please always be sure to acknowledge when something feels right or good. I started to write things down for a short while because I wasn't sure IF "feeling good" was going to happen so I wanted to prove to myself that good things were indeed happening! Keep focused on your intention of "thriving" as your goal, but knowing that on some days you may only feel like you are "surviving". By learning to be okay with that, but not settling into it, good things will continue to happen.

Making PEACE with the empty space within

I am turning 50 this year and while it will be bittersweet for me because we had big plans for 50, the power of love is truly remarkable. I will sometimes have little visions or daydreams that seem to be, what I would say, are ways for Sydney to bring me back to focus or to my present moment. The most recent daydream was my grandmother, who was one of my favoritist people walking the earth, now she is one of my favoritist people in heaven. She is with Sydney dancing around a fire. They are wearing Indian headdresses and smoking a pipe. All I hear is Sydney saying, *"I know momma, smoking isn't good for me. But this is a different kind of smoking. When I smoke this pipe it helps take away your pain."* I get choked up each time something like this happens but it does bring me back to being present in and this new reality.

I think about Sydney constantly and there is nothing I can do about it and I am okay with that. If she isn't in my main thought, I feel her in the back of my mind if that makes sense. Sometimes it happens when I am driving and I fall into doing exactly the opposite of staying present, like I mentioned back in the basic fundamentals, and I hear Sydney's voice saying, *"I'm safe, I'm sorry, I love you"*, just like the day at the morgue. Initially, this reminder would make me feel sick to my stomach because I would recall the morgue and revisit that moment, but over time I am finding ways to stop myself from going back that far and simply focusing on her message. I still get choked up each time it happens, but it is her way of keeping me safe by keeping me present. What beautiful gifts from heaven.

In embracing this new reality, I needed to make peace with the empty space within, the big space that Sydney consumed within my entire being. While she still consumes that space, it initially became the grief cocktail I mentioned earlier. In finding ways to replace that cocktail with all of the things I have mentioned through this book, I am finding ways to live with that empty space and almost treasuring it. The thought of trying to fill it would feel wrong and I also believe impossible. Like a football player's jersey being retired after leaving a team, I am retiring that space and allowing all of the memories, reminders, dreams and reminiscing with others that loved her, to remain in her honor. As time passes, this becomes less like grief for me as I channel the "overflowing" love and energy that could potentially stray to negative. I am sharing this with you in hopes that you will find peace with your empty space.

What's the worst thing that can happen?

Seriously! At this time in your life, and I felt this way so I will say it, can it get any worse? If I really thought about it, sure, it could, but at that particular moment my answer was abso-freaking-lutely not!! But now, being in a more level-headed state of logic, and back in a state of reality, my answer would be different. However, I do not focus on the negative because all of what we have been incorporating along this journey. We want to ensure your new reality is on a stable and secure foundation, and is moving along <u>positively and proactively</u>. (Two of my favorite "P's".) If you continue living the P's, <u>consistently and consciously</u> (two of my favorite C's), no matter what else life has in store for you...wait for it...

You
Will
Have
No
Regrets!

After saying that, keep this in mind: "living in fear or anxiety WILL NOT prevent things from happening" so don't spend your time or energy focusing on them. Lean into the love.

Journal entry from *April 26, 2017*
In memory of Sydney (123 days), in honor of Aubrey & Kevin, and in sharing an incredible living example of all the Core Values I strive to live and share with my clients to "harness the power of love"...

My oldest and beautiful daughter, Aubrey's, wedding anniversary is coming up on May

22nd. Looking back, if I didn't, (AND I ALMOST DIDN'T) practice living our values, we would have had a very different version of what their wedding would have been. You see, when Kevin came to ask me for Aubrey's hand in marriage I said "yes...but in 3 years". I shared with him all MY reasons why they should wait and I believe because of how we (me, the girls and Kevin) communicated and shared, and their trust in my guidance, and me, he lovingly and without hesitation said ok. Remarkable really, when I look back. Well, after we hugged and he left, I put it aside, but something was not sitting well within me.

The next morning I woke as I always do, with a clear head and with the answers of truth, without my ego having a chance to get in the way, and I realized what was not sitting well within me the day before. I was very clearly NOT practicing the core values I had taught my girls and that I believe I practice myself. I just asked my daughter to wait 3 years to marry, put her life on hold because of my insecurities, fears, my "what if's". In that instant I felt shame and immediately knew the plan to right the wrong. I called the kids (because they were kids!!) together and explained to them what I had done and my reasons. I told them if they wanted to get married, then do so! "What's the worst thing that could happen I said!" So the wedding planning began. And in 8 SHORT WEEKS, we had a wedding! Sidebar...I remember when I was proposing a toast to the happy couple, I made a little joke so as to put inquiring minds/assumptions to rest about the rush of the wedding and ensuring everyone that there was "no bun in the oven". But when you're in love, why wait!! Life is short. I had no idea at the time how appropriate a statement that was.

The wedding was outstanding!! We had so many people, family and dear friends, help put the details in place; the food was prepared by our dearest friends, the cupcakes and cake were made by Sydney for her favorite (and only)

The Voice of an Angel

sister and was very excited to be her maid of honor (despite having to wear a long purple dress!) and I had the privilege of walking my sweet daughter down the isle. What a proud moment for me. My girls there together, (almost) all grown up and showing their love to all who were in attendance. It was a simple, yet beautiful event. PERFECT in every way. That was 2 years ago.

Here is the kicker...the realization came to us...came to me, recently that IF I would have not come to my senses and had foregone my core values (out of fear) that I strive to live and teach...we would have had a very different scenario. Asking myself now, "what's the worst thing that can happen"...that would have been if I had enforced the "wait 3 years" rule for marriage, we would not have had Sydney with us May 22, 2017...

A painfully honest admission – I ALMOST made one of the biggest mistakes of my life WHICH

WOULD HAVE BEEN A MAJOR REGRET!!!! I almost allowed my fear of "what if" overshadow my values and who I am.

Please, never let your fears come in the way of how you parent. "Let go" of "their" outcome and allow your children to live as they choose. The choice and consequence is theirs. TRUST IN YOU and your ability to parent and teach (live by example). Communicate unconditionally with those you love. Let them know why you hesitate or decide not to do something so they understand. Be honest with yourself; is that decision for you OR FOR THEM? Spend the time: talking, sharing, and listening. Live by example, not in fear and never judge. And remove the masks; don't worry about what people might think. Do what you feel is best for you and your loved ones. Communicate that with compassion and love, NEVER with ego. Live a life with no regrets...

No regrets, that really pretty much sums it up. Living the P's and the C's above, following the framework I have laid out for you and giving it your "muchness" way of being, you will learn to live a life with no regrets.

Some things to consider for your new reality as you move forward:

♥ Unconditional Communication – let the people you love see your true self, tell them your worst stories as well as your best. Tell them the hard things as well as the easy things. Be real.

♥ Quality time, NOT quantity of time

♥ Be authentic – remove the masks worn with different groups of people. Just be you.

♥ Be honest in every way and with everyone. This creates strong building blocks for all relationships.

♥ Let what feels like it's falling away, fall. Make room for the positive.

♥ Relationships – while they require a level of effort, they should not feel like work. Surround yourself with like-minded people that will always challenge you in positive ways.

♥ Always remember the priorities in life! (people, not stuff!)

♥ Listen completely and allow the white space. Do not always speak.
♥ Break the lineage. Just because it's how your parents did it or it is how you were raised, doesn't make it the only way.

♥ Learn to let go!

♥ Be Strong – this means show and share your emotions.

♥ Have Courage – work through fears, do not let them cripple you or worse, don't impose them upon your children.

♥ Leadership – live each day by example. Strive to be the best you can be, set the example but have zero expectations.

♥ Accountability – it's your responsibility to take care of yourself THEN your raison d'etre, as they are emulating you.

New Reality   Utilize "The List" template to design your new reality for YOU

Conclusion – You did it!

"If we take good care of ourselves, we help everyone. We stop being a source of suffering to the world, and we become a reservoir of joy and freshness." - Thich Nhat Hanh, in *"How to Love"*.

There is a wisdom that I have acquired and incorporated into my new reality since the loss of my daughter. Fortunately, my desire to be in service to others as they find their way through their process has been a gift to me, however, please understand, it is a gift and wisdom I would have preferred not to gain.

I believe that you, too, have the potential to be more than you ever imagined in this lifetime, even after such tragedy. Be kind to yourself, you will fall and sometimes in the heat of emotion you may forget. You will be reminded, nudged, maybe even pushed and you will find your way back to the path you are paving for yourself. In those moments where you feel brought back to the present by something or someone, take those as visits and voices from your Angel. Embrace them and never second-guess them. With the hope of hearing from your baby again and having these moments occur, in time, becomes faith that that is exactly what is happening. Trust and blind faith are things you need to initially fake, I won't lie, but it is worth the risk, and again, what do you have to lose?

New people will come into your life and depending on the Warrior that you choose will determine the type of personality you attract, so be mindful. Like attracts like. Stay true to the warrior within you and you will attract positive people that want to live a good life and turn lemons into lemonade. This is something to monitor and it is not something to feel bad about. You have been through the wringer this last year or so, and others that have grief will feel pulled to you. Show them there is more out there in life and how to bring their Angel with them for the journey in beautiful ways. If they are unable to cross that bridge, that is their journey. Please do not get caught up in trying to fix or heal them. They need to find their way and that is one of the many, many reasons for you to live by example. Many people will look to you; show them what is possible by simply being you.

Communicate your truth; share your true or authentic self, which means being vulnerable. This is something else that feels enhanced for me in this new reality. In remaining as vulnerable as I can with you, there is something I have not yet come to terms with and leaves me a little uncomfortable sharing, but I feel I must. Early on in my first year of losing Sydney, during one of my dreams when she said to share and help people by writing this book, she made a statement that left me cold. She said, *Grief is like sex momma. Sex sells. Well, grief sells too and while it feels dirty saying that, believe me when I say the intention and outcome are completely benevolent.*" Pretty yucky, huh? Well, I have had this in the back of my mind and I suppose not being comfortable with it means I remain altruistic in my cause.

If you have a message to share, do so with absolute conviction and with the purist of intent. If you are like me, you probably are thinking you have been doing this and I am sure you have been. The journey of grief steps up your game and as hard as this is to say, you now have a different voice. I think that might be what Sydney was trying to say about grief "selling". I have noticed that when people find out you have lost a child, they stop for a moment and it's like they put on a different set of ears or maybe they see you in a different light in that split second. **It's at this moment that you have a choice**. With the purist of intent, be that thriving warrior that shares your loss, how this has changed you, show them your grace, and tracks of tears, because it is really unavoidable to try to hide it, and how you hope to continue to find peace. When I do this, I am not "selling", I am being as real and as vulnerable as I am capable, but I believe that sharing this process is a part of my path, my journey. When I believe in something I give it my all, standing on whatever platform I can find to help as many people as possible. Some might consider that "selling". I consider it doing what I was born to do.

Go now, into the world, stand tall knowing you are loved, completely and unconditionally. Go at your pace, in your time and be a warrior. Live each day as you know your sweet baby would want you to and talk to them often. You will never be alone and you will always make them proud and I bet they are saying I love you more right about now. **Lean into that love, always**.

Afterword

Closure, Lack there of & Milestones

This journal entry finds it way here for reasons that relate to the heading of this final chapter and also a heavy realization of karma and literally watching it being "dished out"...

Following the trial, I found myself disappearing into anger and rage. Pieces of me that were beginning to feel whole again felt shattered in unrepairable shards. Me, the person who has always been able to find the silver lining in any situation felt, as if I had finally and truly snapped. As if losing my daughter wasn't tragic enough, to have to relive all of the horror all over again as they tried to determine the fate of another life. The trial quickly goes from a hung jury to a verdict of innocent and I am moved to numbness. More from shock of the theatrics of this outlandish and self serving performance that they refer to as court proceedings.

I sit numb and in disbelief as I watch the judge and jurors and it is so incredibly clear, by behavior & body language, who decided their career or getting home that evening was more important than spending the time to validate the life of a lost beautiful soul.

Looking around the courtroom, I tried to imagine the karma that will be dished out to these unconscious souls more than the outcome of the trial itself. The outcome truly bears no weight for me, as it will not bring my beautiful daughter back to this world, this life. It will however, provide the possibility of opportunity for another, the defendant. This opportunity is what I believe Sydney was preparing me for all of those months as we awaited the trial. That is why I am at such peace with the defendant and surprisingly hold no ill will towards him. I was not prepared, nor did I spend any time lamenting the trial proceedings, the individuals that may be involved or the thought of "what now" once the trial was complete. I was focused on healing within and allowing myself the grace period of pain, as they rehashed the events of that tragic moment that changed the life I loved forever.

Closure

Throughout this entire process of grief, I hear people talk of closure and it hasn't been something I have been able to identify with yet, not in the way I believe they mean closure. While I know everyone has the best of intentions as they try to find words to comfort throughout all of this time, the words now have different meanings or feelings associated with them going forward. If I remember back when Sydney was still with us, closure was something different, lighter somehow. It had no real serious weight and was sometimes anticlimactic and other times celebratory. It was simply the end of something in order to start again with something new.

Closure means bringing to an end, having a conclusion or something that closes or shuts and in my 16 months of living within the grief process and finding my way into the beginning of my new reality, I have experienced closure only twice; the first time being when Sydney died and the second time being the completion of the criminal trial. Neither event came with a sense of relief that it was over, but instead with an incredible feeling of heaviness, emptiness, numbness and with the feeling of "how am I going to move forward?". It has not come with options of how to feel or react or even how to behave, it's as if there is only one outcome to closure after the loss of a child: a very unfortunate revisit to the entire grief process starting with the numbness. For me, the criminal trial brought out all of the exact emotions that the funeral did; and its not that I would have been able to put these words to it back then but now I would describe injustice, being robbed, surreal, unfair, disservice, empty, cheated, hollow and even has twilight zone moments. Being disserved twice in such incredibly tragic ways is a lot for anyone to swallow but ultimately that shitty expression, "it is what it is", which is an "emotional safety" phrase, is all I can offer for moments like those, at least initially, but my goal is to continue through this process and make some more good fuel from all of what I am experiencing.

Some people would say right now that everything happens for a reason, and while I tend to agree with that statement, it is extremely hard to go there at such times of loss. You don't want to believe that there seriously could be a reason for all of this sadness, but as time passes, you never know, you might find things that make some sense. For me, that sense was writing this book for you. It is a way of channeling the anger and turning it to good fuel. I was determined to find good fuel because I instinctively knew how all this could very easily and quickly change me into someone bitter and cold. And there are still days that I really have to focus on the good, my raison d'etre and remind myself why I am still here.

Closure is now, in its most serious state, a true and real form of death and rebirth. Right now, I am unable to see it any other way but perhaps in time it will continue to morph. It's your sweet child's death that ultimately, over time requires your rebirth in order for you to survive. It's part of where the term "new reality" was born. I am not looking to disconnect from all of the good from my life when my daughter was still here walking beside me. I am figuring out how to bring her with me in ways that feel good but, in a life, different than before because that life no longer serves the person I am changed into from my loss. I know you want to do the same.

Lack of Closure

Unanswered questions are lack of closure. There can never be enough closure for you as a momma bear; there will forever be questions that will go without answers or worse, you won't get answers you want to hear or the way you need to hear them. There is absolutely nothing you can do about it, except make the choice to not allow it consume you and slowly kill you.

You have choices, you can allow this to make you a bitter, angry person or you can come to the place where it really does not matter what the answers to any of those questions are because it is not going to bring your baby back. At this point, no amount of detail, answers or time is going to change the outcome to this unfortunate loss and, as I see it, the loss is the only form of complete closure we will experience.

Milestones

As I continue to consider this concept, "milestone", it seems more appropriate and accurate for what happens throughout the grief process. Milestone is defined as progress or development in a significant stage or event in life. If you consider closure vs. milestone as you go through the grief wheel, you never have closure from experiencing anguish or numbness but you have the choice to achieve a milestone of making it out of that stage for a period of time, hoping that each time you experience it, the milestone lasts longer, but that is not closure. I am 16 months into my journey of losing my sweet Sydney and I still have moments of anguish, disbelief and anger. I feel they will always be a part of me but I have the opportunity, or choice, to find my way through them each time they show themselves and that is a milestone.

If you reflect back through the steps of the 6 A's process in Chapter 8, we achieve a milestone at the conclusion of each hurdle from "Acknowledge" to "Adapt" in that process, but there really is no closure. It is simply a milestone that enables you to take a big breath and move forward, slow and steady. Looking farther into the grief process of "Commemorative Tribute", when you set up some form of tribute for your sweet baby, I can assure you that you will experience an array of emotions. As you find your way through them, you will have accomplished milestones, not closure.

My reasoning for this is for clarity and for recognition. Clarity, so you have no confusion as you travel through your tunnel to the light. There are so many people that mean well but don't truly understand what you are going through. They speak and almost provide a sense of false hope around the concept of closure. If you understand the difference between closure and milestone, I believe it will spare you any added grief.

And recognition, in the choice you have made to survive. As you learn how to thrive in your time, show yourself compassion as you travel through this tunnel of grief. When you start to see the light at the other end, take a breath and allow that feeling in: whatever it may be for you. I often times am able to take a little deeper breath or I light the candle we have for Sydney. I thank her for staying close, for steering me and for all the love she had and still has for me. This enables me to find the way to continue to love more, unconditionally, with forgiveness in my heart and believing that karma will have its day.

Peace from the process

There is a thought that keeps popping in my head but I am not exactly sure how to verbalize it, but I will try for you here. Knowing what I believe about heaven and knowing that Sydney was the type of person, when she walked this plane with me, who did not hold grudges, was pure in her thoughts and actions and forgave easily; I believe she is the driving force behind my need and ability to forgive.

I believe that she has complete forgiveness for how tragically she left this earth and for the man that chose to take her trust for granted. I also feel that because of her forgiveness, following the accident, through his injuries and the trial, he has been given a second chance at life. I believe this because she always seemed to see the good in people, even when no one else could. While I may not feel the good she saw in him right now, I, too, believe in second chances, so I hope that Sydney touched him in a way that he wants a better life because I feel like she provided him with the road to do just that.

It's all about making a choice. Just like what you and I need to do now, make a choice, for our sanity, our happiness and for the other people in our lives that love us.

I choose to not allow all of the unanswered questions, the feeling of being cheated by this man and the way it feels the system has failed us, to make me bitter. I choose to follow Sydney's example and keeping with how "we 3" lived our lives together with compassion, love and forgiveness, while having patience with myself, my divine timing for my process through this journey.

My hope for you is that you choose a similar path to:

- ♥ Live with an open heart
- ♥ Stay present
- ♥ Feel the pain
- ♥ Trust your gut

First for yourself and then your family. In your divine time, incorporate the concepts I have shared, to find your way through your grieving process to survive, then thrive. Identify what extraordinary means to you and go live it!! And please, trust that your Angel is guiding and watching over you, always.

Glossary of Terms

Basic Fundamentals – important items for your overall balanced well being during and after this process.

- ♥ Love
- ♥ Raison d'etre
- ♥ Voice of an Angel
- ♥ Staying Present
- ♥ Slowing down and listening
- ♥ Someone you trust
- ♥ Overall wellbeing
- ♥ Be honest with yourself
- ♥ No Regrets

Core Values - what we expect from each other and ourselves. Core Values can help shape your world in altruistic and benevolent ways. They provide direction on how to treat one another.

- ♥ Love
- ♥ Compassion
- ♥ Patience
- ♥ Honesty
- ♥ Forgiveness

Grief Wheel – the steps of the grief process within a dream catcher depicting the negative flows through and away, while the positive lingers and finds it's way down the feathers and into your soul.

Grief Cocktail – is all of the love we have with no place we would really want to direct it anymore, added to all of the other emotions that can often overtake us in an instant and it numbs us.

Guiding Principles - are for decision-making and when consistently applied, aid in ensuring you stay on track in meeting your goals.

- ♥ Identify your raison d'etre
- ♥ Staying present
- ♥ Feel the pain
- ♥ Lean into the love you feel
- ♥ You still have to matter
- ♥ Listen to your gut
- ♥ Be vulnerable
- ♥ Share to heal
- ♥ Detachment

Life over lifelessness - choosing to get back into life in every capacity and at a normal level of passion and muchness.

Muchness - more than life, unique, quirky and extra-ordinary personality.

Pinball Process - fluxing between, and sometimes all at once, shock, pain and anger and then you may branch out to depression but then back again to pain, and maybe reaching hope. It can feel like a pinball machine of emotions, back and forth. I have found that this back and forth and back again, happens well into the 2nd year of grief.

Rifikiness - a Sydney'ism, derived from Lion King. It means extraordinariness with a dash of magic & unusual.

The 6 A's – Acknowledgement, Allowing, Absorption, Acceptance, Adjustment, Adapting

The Warriors

Crusader Warrior - stays sad but has a smile trying to say otherwise, vengeful, becoming bitter not better. Does advocacy work while staying in their pain vs. moving through it and finding peace. The advocacy work is how they appear to be making progress to the outside world but in reality they are reliving their pain and allowing it to become their identity. They stay in pain, don't find complete peace and instead of helping others, rise above their own pain, keep them down with them to suffer silently together.

Surviving Warrior – Survival mode is how these warriors choose to spend their remaining days, surviving but can't seem to move completely through the pain, acknowledging it and any guilt or regrets and allowing them to heal and fall away. These warriors tend to stay sad with good moments, but do no advocacy.

Stays in a place of lackluster and never regain their spark.

Thriving Warrior - Starts in survival mode but realizes there is more in life and that it is okay to want more and goes and finds it. Lives by example and finds how they can reach people to make a difference in the world with the gifts given to them. Accepting and embracing that life can be wonderful, even after the loss of a child.

Grief Process Overview

Utilize "The List" template to design your new reality for YOU

New Reality						
The 6 A's	Acknowledgement	Allowing	Absorption	Acceptance	Adjustment	Adapting
Choose Your Path	Intention	In Your Time	Release	Karma	Crusader Warrior / Surviving Warrior	Thriving Warrior
Guiding Principals	Raison d'être / Staying Present		Feel the Pain / Lean Into What You Love	You Still Have To Matter / Listen To Your Gut	Be Vulnerable / Share To Heal	Detachment
Core Values	Compassion		Patience	Love	Honesty	Forgiveness
Basic Fundamentals	Love / Raison d'être	Voice of an Angel / Staying Present	Slow Down & Listen / Someone You Trust		Overall Wellbeing / Be Honest With Yourself	Service & Hope / No Regrets
Grief Wheel	Shock, Anguish, Denial / Numb		Pain, Guilt, Anger & Regret / Overwhelmed, Sadness, Disbelief		Service & Hope	Define New Reality / Commemorative Tribute

Process Overview

Acknowledgements

Losing a child and the journey through the grief associated with it and everything that follows is never something anyone ever wants to experience in their lifetime. It is also something that I absolutely do not blame a momma bear for ever saying they are grateful it didn't happen to them. I absolutely understand and if for not being where I am, might have said the exact same thing. As a believer in karma and karmic contracts, I am grateful that I was blessed with a heads up on the abbreviated time we would have together in this lifetime. Living mindfully has definitely paid off for me, that is for sure. If I would have had my head in the clouds when my girls were young, our lives most likely would have taken the regular old path vs. the one most don't travel. Our journey together has absolutely been an amazing one. Now I am in the place to understand that while it is still in progress, my team of "we 3" are playing on different planes now with Sydney in heaven.

Since December 24, 2016, my life and the lives of my family, both immediate and extended, have been forever altered. If I had written this about 9 months ago, I would have said my life was over. Now, the only truth to that statement is that my life is over, but only in the way I knew life to be when Sydney was alive. I have taken all of my dreams with Sydney's visits very much to heart and have followed her guidance to the letter. My girls have and always will be my raison d'etre and they are why I found the courage and vulnerability to write this and share, in the hopes that others like us, will create a remarkable life after such a dreadful loss.

So many people have been incredibly kind through these last 16 months and I am and will be forever grateful to them all. I was always that person that handled everything on my own and have been the alpha in most circumstances, so while I was still strong through this time, I learned how to allow someone to help me when I felt like I was falling. My husband has been an absolute earth angel. Breaking all of society's rules around grief, we got married in October 2017 and haven't looked back. It was one of the best things I ever did in my life and both Aubrey and Sydney approve. Sydney did her due diligence on him long before he was given the seal of approval to remain in our lives. Aubrey also happily gave the thumbs up with much less coal raking! You see, back when we first became "we 3", I gave them the key to me. They were permitted to tell me if they didn't like someone I would date and I would always listen. They took this responsibility very seriously and did not play games with it. They understood the magnitude of this charge. When Ken came along, they were very careful to ensure that he was in fact the right man for the job and created a variety of hoops for him to finagle, and he did, with flying colors. I think when he attended Sydney's 21st birthday week in Florida, which was no small feat for him with work and his own children, that he passed all the tests and was deemed a keeper and the one! So to my girls, thank you for loving me and protecting me as much as you do.

Warren Stanley of Stanley Graphic Arts in Harleysville, PA has brought my visions of the cover and graphics to life. He jumped right in to help before he realized the magnitude of the project and it's been amazing to see my visions come to life in such grand ways. Another creative fellow and friend, is Bill Mann, who so kindly shared his channeling with me days after the loss through his beautiful writing. The poem is his ability to be vulnerable and allow others to see his heart through his words. I thank you both sincerely for caring enough, for your vision and your time.

Shout outs also to Judy Lantz for completing some amazing proofreading of this labor of love, Dr. Phyllis Greco Bucci of Holistic Apothecary in Ambler, PA, Kim Cherry of Skippack Acupuncture in Skippack, PA and last but definitely not least, Claudine & Erik Schuster of

Shanteel Yoga Sanctuary of Sellersville, PA. These beautiful people helped make an incredibly challenging time in my life better and even rewarding. Shanteel Yoga Sanctuary has come to play an integral part of my life. The studio was coming to fruition during December of 2017, my "first" at the one-year milestone of living without Sydney. The timing of the studio needing demolition and rebuilding during that time was absolute divine timing! We dove in and did what we could to help and happily worked through the Christmas and New Years Eve festivities so they were ready for business and able to open their doors for January 1st, 2018. The timing of this truly did save my sanity and I am forever grateful.

Claudine and Erik have also dedicated one of the yoga rooms in Sydney's honor with Dr. Seuss quotes all along one wall (picture on next page). We have become family through the process. It is true that *"Family is not just about being from the same tree, it is about the roots*

from many trees that connect, entwine &
nurture."

I would like to thank my book launch team, for going out on a limb, for believing in me and for agreeing to take time out of your busy day to help me, without any idea of what it could possibly entail! You guys rock!

And lastly, to my beautiful daughter, Aubrey, her warrior husband Kevin and my beloved, Ken. Without them, I wouldn't have had a reason to make this journey. Aubrey, I am incredibly proud of how you are handling the loss of your baby sister and of the woman you are becoming. You make your momma proud. Kevin, thank you for taking such incredible care of my beautiful daughter and for always being there. Ken, my gratitude for your unconditional love, compassion and knowing just what to do at every moment, is eternal. Aubrey, Kevin, Ken...

I love you...more.

About the Author

Following the tragic death of her youngest daughter, Marcy remembers hearing Sydney's words within the first month of losing her, *"stay in the pain momma, as hard as that is to do, so your heart stays open and you can feel love..."* Most people don't approach their grief until after the first year.... "I found that for me, and for people like me, that the first year is the most critical time to address the heart, while it is still numb". This book is the process she created in order to live through that horrific experience and find ways to enjoy life again, creating what she calls her new reality, which has reinvigorated her passion for her life long purpose.

How she became who she is today started with a dream when she was very young. Marcy's dream, at that time, was a naïve "call to heal" but it has been an underlying and subconscious motivator for her and who she is becoming. She believes she will always be morphing and growing, which motivates her in bringing that dream to life. Marcy's purpose is to help others become empowered in their lives and live their truest path.

Marcy Stone is a certified and accomplished Intuitive Life Guide for over 15 years and holds advanced training certificates in several healing modalities in addition to having over 17 years of business leadership experience.

As the creator of *The Soulfull Paths® Technique,* she is committed to helping create a world of radiant human beings that are actively manifesting their dreams and gifts into reality.

The Soulfull Paths® technique is a blend of noetic science, applied quantum physics and life force healing. The technique can affect the depths of truth not understood by the intellect, that advance the consciousness and human experience to serve individual transformation, which can also effect our collective transformation.

Holding advanced training in Akashic Records, Theta Healing, Life Force Energy Healing, Hypnosis and she is a Reiki Master, as well as a Certified International Yoga Instructor, Esthetician and Ordained Minister. She is a lifetime student of the healing arts–including meditation, prayer, yoga, and visualization and she brings her passion for growth and self-empowerment into her work and life. Marcy is married to the man of her dreams and has two beautiful daughters, one that walks with her and one that watches over her.

Thank you

To you, so beautiful and devoted to honoring your baby's memory, while believing in what lies ahead can be good. I am proud of you and your will and determination to get to the other end of the tunnel.

To aid in your journey, I am providing a few tools, as well as all of the graphics throughout the book, to assist you. Please click the link below to access them.

- ♥ The List template
- ♥ Color depiction of all graphics
- ♥ 3 poems with words of comfort

Go to www.marcystone.com/thrivingwarriors. I hope they are helpful as you create your new reality.

There is also a Q&A page on my website that is private and available to you, if you need an ear or have a question, please feel comfortable and know that you will not be judged. We all walk this walk differently and I honor and respect that.

May you always lean into the love, find peace and live an extraordinary life.

Made in the USA
Middletown, DE
14 December 2020

27934566R00152